Think Like a Cartoonist™

FOR
Carol & WAYNE!

WISHING YOU MUCH
LAUGHTER & INSpiration!

, 2024

Think Like a Cartoonist™

A CELEBRATION OF HUMOR AND CREATIVITY

Leigh Rubin and Friends

RIT Press
Rochester, New York

Published and distributed by:
RIT Press
90 Lomb Memorial Drive
Rochester, New York 14623
https://press.rit.edu

Printed in the United States of America

ISBN 978-1-956313-04-8 (print)
ISBN 978-1-956313-05-5 (electronic)

Library of Congress Control Number: 2023944845

We gather on the traditional territory of the Onöndowa'ga:' or "the people of the Great Hill." In English, they are known as Seneca people, "the keeper of the western door." They are one of the six nations that make up the sovereign Haudenosaunee Confederacy.

We honor the land on which RIT was built and recognize the unique relationship that the Indigenous stewards have with this land. That relationship is the core of their traditions, cultures, and histories. We recognize the history of genocide, colonization, and assimilation of Indigenous people that took place on this land. Mindful of these histories, we work towards understanding, acknowledging, and ultimately reconciliation.

For Teresa—
Thank you for all the joy, laughter, love, and inspiration.

"Welcome back, sir. Are you planning on being our guest for one night only, or will this be your usual extended stay?"

Contents

Foreword

BUILDING A CREATIVE COMMUNITY CULTURE THROUGH A CARTOONIST-IN-RESIDENCE

James J. Winebrake

How do you build a creative community culture? How do you inspire people to actively engage in creative thought? How do you encourage the exploration of creative solutions to complex problems? How do you build creative policies that allow our social, educational, and political institutions to thrive?

These were the issues I was wrestling with as the dean of the College of Liberal Arts at Rochester Institute of Technology (RIT) in 2017. At RIT we talked a lot about "creativity." In fact, it was a hallmark of the RIT "brand." But how creativity influenced, and manifested itself in, the work we did as teachers and learners was still nebulous and vague.

I believe that everyone has "creative" capabilities. But certainly, some people are more talented at thinking creatively than others. What is their secret? How do they find solutions to problems that no one else would have ever thought of? What is their thought process, and what other skills and techniques do they use to apply this creative capacity?

These questions led me on a course of action to *intentionally* develop novel ways to promote creativity and illustrate how different tools used by creative thinkers and doers could be used to help us expand our own creative capacity. But in terms of *how* to do this, I was stuck.

Then, along came Leigh Rubin. Although I was already a big fan of *Rubes*®, the cartoon that Leigh had in syndicated newspapers nationally, I was formally introduced to Leigh by a mutual friend, Thom Worden. Thom had known Leigh for some time and spoke often about Leigh's ability to talk about creativity to audiences in interesting ways.

So, I emailed Leigh. And, happily, he emailed back. And a relationship developed that I knew would be rewarding for RIT and for me—and, hopefully, for Leigh.

It was in one of our early conversations that I said something to the effect of: "Many universities have scholars-in-residence. Or musicians-in-residence. Or artists-in-residence. But, what about a cartoonist-in-residence?" Leigh let out with an enthusiastic, "Sure, that sounds cool!" Our brainstorming began.

We took that simple concept—a "cartoonist-in-residence" at a major national university—and outlined what the activities of that position would entail. We brainstormed about lectures, and cartooning demonstrations, and public events, and discussions on how a cartoonist thinks. We believed that in sharing his creative thought process with students, faculty, staff, and the community, Leigh could influence how his audience could solve problems in their own personal and professional spheres.

Subsequent to those planning conversations in 2018, Leigh was appointed RIT's official "cartoonist-in-residence," beginning in the 2018–2019 academic year, and that appointment was extended for several years afterward. As RIT's cartoonist-in-residence, Leigh has touched the lives of hundreds of students, faculty, and staff. He has lectured to students who range from artists to engineers and communication majors to philosophy majors—and his lectures always include a lot of laughs as he talks about approaches he has used to stretch his mind and the minds of his readers. He has also shared his creative skillset with faculty, who have employed his approaches to creativity to design their own lectures and even new courses and programs. And he has given public addresses and interviews that share this creative recipe with the larger community.

The "cartoonist-in-residence" was a concept that evolved through a creative process. We took two worlds—one of the cartoonist and one of the academic—and demonstrated that when looked at through a certain lens, these seemingly different environments had a lot in common. We are hopeful that this is a concept that could be implemented in many different ways (A "jam band-in-residence"? A "stand-up comic-in-residence"? A "magician-in-residence"?) to further the exploration of creativity in an academic environment. We plan on continuing conversations at other universities to further this idea nationally.

James J. Winebrake is currently the provost at the University of North Carolina Wilmington and was the dean of the College of Liberal Arts at RIT when Leigh Rubin became RIT's cartoonist-in-residence. In between laughing hysterically at *Rubes*® cartoons, Dr. Winebrake conducts research on clean transportation and attempts to catch redfish on the fly in the marshes of North Carolina—usually unsuccessfully.

Acknowledgments

A very special thanks to Bruce Austin, Jamie Winebrake, Thom Worden, Alexandra Hoff, Marcia Trauernicht, Laura DiPonzio Heise, Marnie Soom, Sue Weisler, Anne Cook, Eric C. Wilder, Molly Cort, Steven Bradley, Jim Holodak, Stephanie Pottick, Robin Blakely, and all my family and friends who contributed to this project, whether published or not, who have been with me on this continuing creative journey.

Introduction

Leigh Rubin

Life constantly challenges us. Great or small, it tests our imaginations and our ability to be creative.

As a professional cartoonist, I face a daily situation: create a fresh, funny, and often just plain silly, illustrated gag. Once a week I submit seven cartoons to my syndicator. They, in turn, transmit the cartoons to a variety of newspapers and other media outlets that publish my work.

"Dot-connecting" is one method I use to solve this relentless demand for creativity. Somewhat random, and decidedly nonformulaic, dot-connecting brings together multiple, often unrelated, subjects with the goal of having them coalesce into something entirely new. This freedom inspires the flow of creativity without commitment or restriction until just the right combination of art and humor find each other, resulting in a "perfect" marriage.

But dot-connecting is not my only method. I'll often ask myself a question and see how many ways there are to answer it, sometimes changing the question a bit so as to allow for more possible answers. For example, instead of asking *why* the chicken crossed the road, I'll ask, "How many ways *can* a chicken cross the road?"

Another method is bending—without breaking—the "rules." That is, pushing or stretching the boundaries of our collective "reality" just far enough, while remaining relatable and without confusing or losing the audience. What comedians call, "reading the room." Imagine conceiving and executing a hilarious cartoon, only to have my wife or a friend stare blankly at my proud achievement. Or worse—give it a polite "courtesy" laugh. Laughing at your own jokes is acceptable only when you are the only one in the "comedy club." But your career in stand-up will be limited at best.

Both asking questions and bending the rules afford the luxury of flexibility. And flexibility provides me with the necessary lubrication for the creative gears to get turning.

Creativity is imagination put into action. Whether it's quickly handling an unforeseen situation, dreaming up a new piece of art, or applying a skill in an unusual or a different way. There is something inherently rewarding about being creative.

Successful people achieved their success by overcoming challenges. These challenges test their creative ability. Their stories can inspire us. And more important for this book's purposes, their stories are particularly instructive for the imaginative and creative ways those successful people solved their challenges.

All the more reason to read the pages that follow. Dot-connecting, the bumper-sticker "summary" I use to describe my main method of creativity, is not idiosyncratic, even as its precise application may very well be.

When I first met with this book's publisher, instead of the autobiographical approach I was taking, he suggested developing the project by enlisting a journalist as a coauthor. Journalists are accustomed to reaching out to people from a variety of backgrounds to learn their views. Sometimes, maybe often, perfect strangers! Maybe following that procedure would demonstrate how others creatively solved problems. In other words, how non-cartoonists "think like cartoonists."

Though journalists may be underpaid, they rarely like to work for free. And since I had no budget to hire one, I would be the person to reach out.

Happily, many answered my call.

During the course of a year I called, emailed, and texted more than 150 acquaintances, friends, and family and asked (some might say *bothered, badgered, annoyed,* or *cajoled*) them to send an anecdote explaining how they came up with a creative solution to a problem. What were the dots, and how did they connect them?

Often, the stories were delightfully entertaining. But more important, their anecdotes were *applicable, instructive, enlightening*, and, most of all, they were examples of how seeing the world imaginatively produced pleasing results.

In each instance, the writer was thinking like a cartoonist.

To organize the essays, I turned to the Boy Scouts for help. A dozen principles form the Scout Law: "A Scout is Trustworthy, Loyal, Helpful, Friendly, Courteous, Kind, Obedient, Cheerful, Thrifty, Brave, Clean, and Reverent."

Cartoonists, being economical ("lazy"), require only ten. To "Think Like a Cartoonist," one must be Adaptable, Disciplined, Resourceful,

Persistent, Observant, Unflappable, Unpredictable, Optimistic, Imaginative, and Irreverent.

While a good sense of humor may keep us internally, if not eternally, young, humor may not always be the answer, part of the answer, or even appropriate to any given situation. But I believe being open to the humorous, the irreverent, and the silly is important. Humor may be a universal language, but everybody speaks it differently.

The pages that follow illustrate (ahem) the variety and diversity of dot-connecting methods people from many walks of life used to creatively approach a broad and deep range of situations—from the seemingly trivial and insignificant to the apparently monumental and overwhelming.

Sue Lutz, for instance, solved a hospital's bureaucratic mistake by combining "innocent" fumbling and a cup of coffee; read her essay, *Clumsiness and Caffeine*. Or take a look at *Diamond Rings and Knuckleheads* to see the clever way Rick Rittenberg coupled his knowledge of the unaligned disciplines of geology and motorcycles during a job interview in a last-ditch attempt to gain much-needed employment. In Jeff Harman's *Bikers and Baseball*, you will learn how a highway patrolman diffused a potentially violent situation by drawing on a childhood lesson he learned from a Los Angeles Dodger. Margaret Morrison spotted the aesthetic beauty of a berry-stained napkin and turned it into a prize-winning piece of art.

What all the writers featured between these covers share is a "virtue by negation." None grab for the lowest-hanging fruit. Although for some comedians—and cartoonists—knee-level seems their highest stretch for the easiest pun. Admittedly occasionally hilarious, if only after a few drinks, they are, to the sober, eye-rollers.

I try to never underestimate the intelligence of my readers. Sometimes (perhaps often) deeper, more layered, and nuanced wordplay offers them a more rewarding, memorable experience. It takes the simple pun from groan-inducing to grin-producing. Part of this approach insists that readers connect the dots for themselves. The more readers are invested in the cartoon, the more devoted they become. Sometimes the result is that some readers may not get the gag immediately. But so what if it takes two seconds or two weeks? Eventually, if it is good, the gag will be gotten. Then it is pure magic. Cartoonists who stretch their own imaginations require readers to stretch theirs.

Now it's your turn. Start anywhere. Randomly flip to any page, and see if these stories spark your imagination and creativity—and maybe even inspire you to Think Like a Cartoonist!

Bending the Rejection Rules
GOOD NEWS, BAD NEWS
Leigh Rubin

On the bookshelf in my office is a binder. No ordinary binder, the *Binder of Rejection*. Inside are dozens of letters, some personally written and some form letters, all on the same "theme." For some reason or another, my work did not suit their "editorial needs" at a given time. The rejections came from every major and some minor syndicates—the companies that market and sell cartoons and other features to newspaper and magazine editors. The reasons didn't really matter; all gave me the thumbs-down. One rejection letter even came from a syndicate I didn't write to directly: A newspaper editor who liked my work had submitted to a syndicate on my behalf.

But stories of successful authors rejected dozens of times are plentiful. Maybe that's the only thing I have in common with such literary luminaries as Dr. Seuss and J.K. Rowling.

Sometimes the quest for success might require a bit of creative mischief—by turning a rejection into an acceptance.

Now, I'm not particularly proud of this (well, maybe just a bit), but technically it's still within the bounds of honesty, with just a touch of entering one of those "gray areas."

One rejection letter was from a well-known West Coast feature syndicate. This carefully written rejection was complimentary and extremely frustrating.

The first complimentary bit was as follows: "Although your work is in many ways the equal of features already in syndication"—*so far, so good, until...*"it has one *problem*." (Non-form rejection letters almost invariably say, "*It has one problem.*")

Now for the frustrating part: "Features currently in syndication have the special advantage of being known quantities with following and track records. To compensate for not having such advantages, a new feature must be absolutely outstanding, and very few new features are absolutely outstanding." *Here's another complimentary bit:* "Thus, although your work is unquestionably above almost all other submissions—thousands of them (*now back to the bad bit*)—we nevertheless find ourselves unable to syndicate it."

Leech comedy clubs

So the letter says you have to be already known (aka, famous and successful), but how do you get famous and successful if you are just starting out? No feature ever started out as a known quantity. They all had to develop followings. Frustrating, yes, but that letter did provide me with the following quote, which I used on my future promotional materials:

"Unquestionably a cut above."—*Big West Coast Newspaper Syndicate*

The good part was that my promo material got noticed. The bad part was that it was noticed by the person who wrote the letter, who then gave me a call to express his displeasure. It was a somewhat uncomfortable call. If only caller ID had been available in 1985.

Whether you are a writer, cartoonist, or creative in *any* field, rejection goes with the territory. How many writers, actors, composers, and inventors have been turned down over and over again, and it's only through sheer dogged persistence that they hadn't given up? We may never know how many great stories, songs, movies, or inventions never saw the light of day because their creators were too thin-skinned about rejection. The media loves to focus on stories of the supposed "overnight success." But in reality, most overnight successes happen over many, many nights. Good things may come to those who wait, but, unfortunately, some writers and artists achieve their greatest successes posthumously, or, in the case of a humorist or cartoonist...posthumorously. Oh well, you know what they say: "Better late than never."

3

Clumsiness and Caffeine

Susan Lutz

It was around 1983, and I was employed in the cardiac-care unit of a Long Island, New York, hospital.

A new patient (I'll refer to him as "Mr. B") was behaving in a particularly loud, overbearing, and critical manner. Recognizing that patients often feel vulnerable and perceive a loss of control—which can have a negative impact on their emotions—we implemented a care plan that included the goal of gaining his trust. This was quite a challenge. Mr. B. believed that someone would be careless or make an error that would harm him. He expressed anger when a breakfast tray lacked the specific juice he'd ordered; this simple human error was easily resolved by his nurse, yet it reinforced his belief. He kept a notebook in which he recorded the names of and his interactions with each person who entered his room. Staff members felt rather intimidated by these behaviors.

After a few days, we needed his signature consenting to an invasive heart procedure. The document is preceded by a full explanation by the physician, and the patient has the opportunity to ask questions before deciding whether or not to sign. Usually within an hour a patient would notify their nurse to witness the signature. In this case it was more than a full day, during which nurses spent significant time explaining details and contacting the physician to meet with the patient again. Finally, the consent was completed and delivered to the unit secretary, who then used a flat ink roller (1980s' technology) to imprint the patient's embossed hospital ID plate on it for inclusion in his record. Imagine our dismay when we discovered she had imprinted the form with the wrong ID.

It was against policy to maintain an altered consent, so we needed a new one. No one wanted to explain this to Mr. B., but I was the "charge nurse" and so ...

Delaying the confrontation for a few minutes while I drank coffee, I came up with an idea. Although this anxious man had no tolerance for the slightest human error, maybe he would accept another type of human frailty.

I poured my coffee over the consent while staff looked at me as though I'd lost my mind. I hurried to Mr. B.'s room with the soaked form and dramatically exclaimed, "Oh, I'm so sorry! I can't stand being clumsy! Look at what happened: I spilled coffee on your consent!" He calmly dismissed my concern and told me he'd sign a new copy. I had correctly surmised that he could accept a klutz.

Susan Pfleegor Lutz, **RN**, **BSN**, began her career in critical care on Long Island, New York, and relocated to Maryland some years ago. She then found fulfillment in a new area of specialty as a school nurse/case manager. Now retired, Susan enjoys hiking, birdwatching, and other pursuits with family and friends, yet still finds time for daily ice-cream research. Results will be published when she tires of tasting new flavors. Susan extends an invitation to her cousin Leigh to join her research project.

Hot Water and Horoscopes

Linda Warner

Everyone has a day of reckoning at some time in their career.

I'm talking about the day you do something so unforgivable that you might be censured, demoted, or fired. My day came when I pulled the comics page from our local paper.

As the night editor, I had the final say as to what ran in our paper the next day. Major stories that had been decided upon by the editorial staff were a given. Lesser items were subject to my decision. So, when the ad-department rep came to my desk in a panic, on deadline, and explained how a full-page ad had been overlooked when the paper was laid out, it was my job to decide which page to pull.

My choices were the editorial page or the comics. As a writer, I believed the editorial page was sacred. This was where my editor wrote opinions on the antics of politicians and governing bodies, on whether or not a proposition should be approved, and on laws and lawbreakers. The comics page, on the other hand, was just the comics. Boy, was I wrong.

I knew something was amiss when I entered the front office the next day. Phones were ringing incessantly, and I was receiving glares from several of the office staff. When my editor greeted me at my desk by asking, "What were you thinking when you pulled the comics page?" I realized I had somehow made a grave error.

The phone-call deluge had begun as soon as the office opened that day. According to my editor, most calls began with, "Mind you, I don't believe in them, but what happened to the horoscopes?" Seems that no one in our valley could get through the day without finding out what the day was going to be like. Guess I was the exception. If I could have foreseen this traumatic event, I would have called in sick.

Fast-forward several years. The events of that day were forever seared into my brain, and once again I had a decision to make while on deadline. Somehow the daily horoscopes had been lost, and no one had noticed until about an hour before deadline. Usually the page was pasted up from syndicated copy and sent to camera before I got in. But someone on the day shift had forgotten to pass along the message about the missing horoscopes, and I had inherited the gaping hole on the page that had been set aside in a corner of the composing room. Worse yet, the composing room boss was telling me to come up with copy to fill the hole or he would slap a house ad—an ad touting the benefits of classified ads or subscribing to the paper—on the page.

I went back to my desk in a panic. No one wanted to bring down the wrath of the horoscope gods. After very little discussion, my assistant and I decided there was only one thing to do. We would write the horoscopes ourselves—but with a twist.

We composed a list of all the birthdays of our coworkers and divided it. If we got along well with a fellow journalist, he or she would receive a favorable horoscope, but those on our naughty list would not be as lucky. The only exception was my daughter's horoscope. She was job hunting and needed good karma. Mind you, we never wished evil on anyone, just warnings of possible car trouble or cautions about work- or romance-related activities. As for my daughter, she received a prediction of success through changing job opportunities. Our work was done. Our deadline was met.

As I entered the front office the next day, I found everything was relatively quiet.

No phones were ringing off the hook, no one was glaring at me, and no editor met me with, "What were you thinking ...?" The only person to have mentioned the horoscopes was my daughter. She had gone off to her first real job interview—one that did not involve flipping burgers—with a positive attitude and a smile on her face. She had informed me as she was leaving that her horoscope had said that job possibilities were looking good.

Linda Warner got her start in journalism at a small family-owned newspaper chain in northeastern Ohio. From there she worked her way through several positions, eventually ending up at a growing newspaper in Southern California. She has a way of getting into strange predicaments, so the Sports Department staffers would play the theme from "I Love Lucy" for her from time to time. After 20 years in journalism, she left to become a teacher. True to form, Linda checked the wrong box at a teacher-recruitment event and, instead of becoming a sixth-grade teacher, she became a special-ed teacher.

The Element of Surprise

Leigh Rubin

There's almost nothing I like more than the "Thrill of Getting Away with It."

I'll clarify.

I love a *good* practical joke, not the kind where someone is hurt. The kind that is sneaky and clever and where, after the "big reveal," everyone, including the intended "beneficiary" of the joke, has a good laugh.

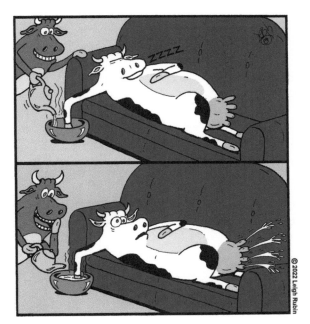

The same goes when creating a really good gag.

Creating a really good gag is definitely more art than science, and depending on the gag, it should contain at least some, if not all, of the following ingredients in varying amounts: smarts, artfulness, cleverness, silliness, mischief, humor, absurdity, anticipation, imagination, and timing.

Late one evening in the physics lab, with a little help from a colleague, Professor Rittenberg discovers the element of surprise.

Putting just the right measure of these ingredients into a cartoon will give the reader a memorable and enjoyable surprise.

Overcoming temptation, David opted against the obvious, unsportsmanlike cheap shot.

Knowing how far you can push the boundaries of "getting away with it" and judging where to stop and allow the reader's imagination to take over is a developed skill. The trick is to be able to put your funniest foot forward without crossing the line. Oh, and be sure to watch your step.

Punguins and Vice Cream

Phil Yeh and Leigh Rubin

In 1986, Leigh Rubin and I were about to go on the road with other cartoonists R. C. Williams and Wally Davis to promote literacy using humor and cartoons. We called our campaign "Cartoonists across America." On the way back from the first leg of the trip—which took us up the West Coast into British Columbia and, eventually, through thirty-two states and two Canadian provinces—we thought about creating a book that addressed the literacy issue through humor. Leigh was always quick to come up with witty puns, and my area of expertise was making up characters to tell a story. Leigh created the lead characters, brothers Penguin and Pencilguin, when we were visiting my friends John and Michele Wozniak in San Francisco. Michele collected penguins. Once we had these two title characters, with their noses a pen and a pencil, the rest of the characters came easily. Leigh

came up with the bad guys, Swordfish and Sore Mussel. They were against reading.

The key to telling this story was making it about teaching people to learn to read in a non-judgmental way. We did this by creating a literacy center in the town of Penguin City in the South Pole. The literacy tutor was Auntie Arktic. Her student was an adult penguin named Punguin, which was perfect for Leigh's puns. Punguin's best line was, "Take my ice, please." His career included writing for the legendary comedian Henny Younguin.

We also created an ice-cream shop run by the penguin brothers' father, whose name was Dadguin. This allowed Leigh's imagination to run wild creating all these fish-flavored ice-cream delights such as Strawberry Starfish and Peanut Butter and Jellyfish. Dadguin's favorite saying was, "Without reading, life would be a 'Rocky Road.'"

On the southern leg of our "Cartoonists across America" tour, Leigh and I temporarily split with the other cartoonists and flew to Florida to speak at the National Adult Continuing Education Conference in Miami.

After picking up our rental car, we headed to the conference.

In the trunk of the car we had foam-core cutouts of our penguin characters that we planned to use during our presentation at the convention.

At the time, *Miami Vice* was a huge hit TV show, and I jokingly thought that it would be cool if we got to see the show being filmed. As we were driving by a store in Miami, we spotted a TV crew setting up; we stopped and found out that they were actually filming an episode of *Miami Vice!*

The store was still open, since the filming hadn't yet started. That's when one, or both, of us—I can't quite recall—had an audacious idea. *What if we could get one of our cartoon characters into the store window in time for the filming of one of the biggest shows in America?!*

We popped open the trunk, grabbed "Glenguin," the punk-rocker penguin guitarist cutout, and quickly headed into the store.

Now all we had to do was convince the store clerk to let us place our character in the window. But how?

As it turned out, the clerk didn't speak much English and we didn't speak much Spanish, but we said we were cartoonists, and he said, "Cartoonist, like Charles Schulz?" and we said "Yes, just like Charles Schulz." (Except we were broke and not famous, but that didn't seem particularly relevant enough to mention at the time.)

Glenguin and friends as seen on season three, episode ten, "Streetwise," of Miami Vice. Courtesy of Phil Yeh.

Apparently, Charles Schulz's name carried a lot of weight, and the clerk happily allowed us to place our cartoon in the window just in time for the filming.

As far as I know, Glenguin became the only cartoon penguin to ever "guest-star" on the show.

After the tour was over, we published *Penguin and Pencilguin* as a 96-page trade paperback in 1987. It sold out.

As a nod of thanks to Miami Vice, Phil and Leigh pose as Miami Vice's Crockett and Tubbs.

Later we published eight issues of comic books starring Penguin and Pencilguin. We continued to play off puns with titles for stories like "Peter Punguin," "Don Guinote," "Miami Ice," "King Arthur's Quart," and "The Wizard of Ice." The books addressed the serious subject of illiteracy by using humor.

Phil Yeh began drawing at the age of two in 1956. His dad was an engineer and gave him unlimited paper on which to express his creativity. He moved on to publishing his own work in high school, with his friend Mark Eliot, with a little humor magazine called *Cement*. In 1973, Eliot and Yeh would start their own newspaper, *Uncle Jam*, which covered health, books, the arts, and travel. Phil has dabbled in radio, film, cartoons, painting, and a number of other stuff throughout his life. In 1985, he formed Cartoonists across America with a few cartoonist friends, including Leigh Rubin. In 1990, they added *And the World* to their banner. To date, the group has painted more than 2000 murals in forty-nine US states and eighteen countries. He has written approximately 100 books and painted a lot of pictures. Phil's life is made entirely possible through the help of Linda Yeh. There's more at www.wingedtiger.com.

Hospice and Humor

Sam White

I am a hospice chaplain. I am also a cartoonist. While my strip appears in four newspapers, it is through hospice that I make my living. When people ask me how I can do the hospice job, I sometimes tell them I do it to support my cartooning habit. This generally leads to more explanation than they, or I, want, so I don't say it often.

Most people have had some dealings with hospice, and they ask how I can do it—because they can't imagine doing it. Their previous experience with hospice was sad, and it ended in death, so how could I possibly do that over and over?

It ain't easy. And I have a lot of ex-coworkers to back me up on that. Good nurses and health aids and social workers and other chaplains who came to hospice because they thought they could really do some good, or they felt called, or they just didn't read the ad right. But then

the reality sunk in: Everyone we work with is on hospice because they are dying, and most of them do.

(Yes, I said "most." You see, one of the things hospice does is provide an environment in which the patient can, hopefully, live out their last days comfortably. Some, in this process, actually get better and are removed from our service. They might be back one day, but for now they have—as we say—"graduated." We rejoice in those moments.)

So there you are, with a patient you have gotten close to because you have been seeing them regularly for weeks or months (or in some cases, *years*), and the awaited day comes. And you cry along with the family because you are losing a friend. You hug everybody and pray with them and tell the same old stories one more time... and then you go back out to your car and compose yourself because you have to drive across town or a block away and cheerfully tend to another friend who is dying. Some professionals find out quickly that they can't handle that and return to whatever job they had before.

And I may one day, too, since it does take a toll on a person.

Still, it is rewarding. As a chaplain, I remember a man I was asked to visit, who hadn't said anything in four days nor opened his eyes in that time. His sisters and his mother were gathered in his room at the care home. I invited the family to join hands with me, and we gathered around the patient's bed as I said a prayer. I had just finished the prayer when the patient said, in a deep, booming voice—without ever opening his

eyes—"Amen!" He died the next day without ever having said another word.

Or the patients I have been singing old hymns to who can't say an intelligible sentence, but they suddenly sing along on "Amazing Grace" or "Old Rugged Cross." One time, twenty or more patients in an Alzheimer's wing started singing along, and we did several tunes together. Did I mention that I'm not a particularly good singer? It didn't matter. It was the words and the old tunes that literally struck a chord with those wonderful old minds.

Now, having read this far, you may be wondering where hospice intersects with cartooning. There are two ways, in fact. One is that many

of my patients are very hard of hearing. Some of them even have a white board or a large tablet and a marker with which to write questions. One day it was a patient's birthday, and rather than writing out "Happy Birthday," I drew a cake with candles. Just a simple, quick line drawing, but the patient loved it. Soon I was drawing cats and dogs, and she was telling me about her pets. I drew a Bible on another visit, and she told me how much she loved to read the Bible and wished she could still hear sermons. I have since developed somewhat of a repertoire of simple objects I can draw quickly in order to spark conversation.

But the other way my cartooning has intersected (and even helped) with hospice is back at the office. By rule, we have to meet every four-

teen days and discuss each and every patient. Now, I can't stand any kind of meeting, but as you can imagine, a meeting where all you are discussing are dying patients and their symptoms can become pretty grim. Human nature being what it is, though, there's some gallows humor (death-bed humor?) that goes on in there that would probably mortify the outside world. Everyone takes part, but I'm the only one (at our hospice, anyway) who illustrates their jokes. I've been able to give the room a well-timed laugh with cartoons about deep-vein thrombosis and squamous-cell carcinoma; I even once brought the room down with a cartoon that linked bladder spasms to our local minor-league baseball team. (Most of these ideas get reworked and show up later in my comic strip, and I am grateful no one was there for the conversation that inspired it!)

Now that (as of this writing) Covid-19 has us working from home, I have to attend the meeting remotely.

While everyone reports in over the phone about their patients, I'm the only one who is also expected to text a cartoon to everyone in the meeting.

Sam White learned to read by having the "funnies" read to him from the paper each evening. That's also how he learned to draw and where his lifelong ambition of being a newspaper cartoonist came from. To support his cartooning habit, he has worked as a hospice chaplain, preacher, software tester, copywriter, author, and dreamer.

Observe What Isn't There

Leigh Rubin

How do you "see" what isn't there? The trick is keeping your literal eyes *and* your "imaginative" eyes open.

Inspiration is all around us, just begging to be noticed, but only the literal world will be seen if you are just looking with your physical peepers. See with your eyes. Observe with your imagination.

I was taking a July road trip with a friend to visit another buddy who lives in Oregon. The drive is more than a thousand miles, so we split the trip into two days.

The halfway point is Red Bluff, a town in Northern California that is just shy of three hours south of the Oregon border.

We checked into our hotel, and on the way to our rooms, I noticed a carefully constructed orb-spider web spanning a circular opening on the front of one of the hotel's outdoor lights, about six inches from the exposed bulb. It was an ingenious place for a spider's web, since with so many flying insects zipping about, once the light was switched on, a summer-evening bug buffet was all but guaranteed.

Was the placement of the web just random, or was it purposeful? I like to imagine the latter.

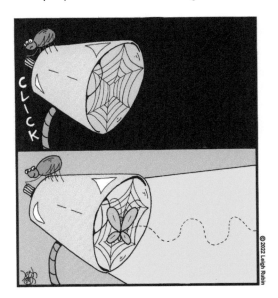

Holes and Holiness

Dave Wesley

I was seven years old.

One otherwise ordinary Sunday at our house, five kids, Mom, and Dad, piled into the station wagon and headed to church. We listened to Mom's favorite religious programs on the radio: "The Old Fashioned Revival Hour" and "The Hour of Decision." On these Sunday trips, we frequently heard the beginning of a third program*, which was heralded by the anthem "Lift up the Trumpet." The trumpet announced to us that we were late. This day, though, there was no trumpet. We were on time.

My dad joined the other deacons in preparing for the morning services. I tagged along. When we got to the small cottage on church property that had been repurposed for Sunday school and meeting rooms, we faced a quandary.

"Who's got the key?" "Anybody got the key?" Questions in rapid succession were followed by answers, none resolving the problem.

The door was locked, and they couldn't get in. "Joe, I thought it was your turn to bring the key." "Nope, my turn was last week. I think it's Don's turn this week." "Don's not here." "Oh. Would anyone else have a key? Or know where one is?" "Fred, I thought you had a spare key." "Nope. Not anymore." And on it went. For several minutes.

Meanwhile, I wasn't looking for a key. I was thinking about how to get into the house. I just looked at that door, and suddenly it hit me. I thought it was so obvious that surely one of these men would figure it out. But all I heard was more of, "If we can't find the key, how are we going to get in?"

Like I said, I wasn't looking for a key. I was staring at the door. Claiming I prayed and miraculously got the answer might have seemed appropriate under the circumstances, but it would have been a lie. Besides which it didn't occur to me. Instead, staring at the door from my seven-year-old height, I could clearly see a way in. This was an old door, the bottom half of which was composed of 4 x 4 in. panels. And the panel right in front of me was missing. There was a hole. Right next to the doorknob.

A small voice (I would have said a "still, small voice," this being at church and all; however, it was just my small voice) somehow cut through the blizzard of adult questions and was heard to say, "Why don't you just reach in and open the door?" Patiently, the adult voices of the deacons explained to the seven-year-old that the door couldn't be opened because they didn't have a key. Pointing at the missing panel, I repeated, "Why don't you just reach in and open the door?"

Jaws dropped and hands collided as they reached through the hole. The door was unlocked. The day was saved. Saved for everyone but my dad, that is. Since he was an engineer, he took some good-natured ribbing from the other deacons. "Bob, you need your seven-year-old son to help you figure out how to open a door?" And so forth. Of course, none of them had fig-

ured it out, either. I think this was just their way of trying to save face.

But that didn't stop them from coming up with stories about how unusual, creative thinking had solved many problems. Like the truck driver who let the air out of his tires so he would fit under the overpass. All of a sudden they were full of creativity. Just not as quickly as the seven-year-old.

If there's a moral to the story, I guess it would be: By focusing all your attention on making one particular solution work, you might be missing the obvious—the one that's right in front of you.

No, wait. That's not it. The moral to the story is: Don't bring your precocious seven-year-old with you when problem-solving with your peers.

*For anyone interested, "Lift up the Trumpet" heralded *The Voice of Prophecy* with H. M. S. Richards Sr., a program tracing its roots back to 1929 and still on the air today. *The Old Fashioned Revival Hour* was Charles E. Fuller's program. Another early broadcaster, he was a founder of the Fuller Theological Seminary. *The Hour of Decision* was Billy Graham's radio program.

"As you can see, son, simplicity is the key."

Dave Wesley finds himself retired after forty-some years in the newspaper business. In addition to enjoying three grandchildren with his wife, Jane, he serves as a stakeholder on American Cancer Society Research committees. Dave enjoys old movies and watching baseball, even though he wasn't very good at it. (Years after his Little League experience, his dad told him the reason he put Dave at second base was because he couldn't throw the ball far enough to get it in play from right field.)

Whales and Tails

Leigh Rubin

My wife and I are fortunate enough to live near Pismo Beach, one of the very few remaining strips of California coastline where you can drive right on to the beach and, for those more adventurous, drive *into* the surf. We also enjoy Scrabble®, and rather than sit at home and play, we'll often take our red, aging Land Cruiser to the coast, park on the sand, roll down the windows, and experience the smell of the fresh ocean breeze.

It's a relaxing way to spend the afternoon, watching pelicans perform their incredible Olympian vertical high dives for anchovies, sardines, and any other seafood delicacies they can scoop up.

Or the seagulls that repeatedly perform their version of "catch and release" as they pluck clams from the shoreline, hover fifteen or twenty feet off the dense, hard-packed sand closest to the surf, then drop them until they crack open—where inside a tasty morsel awaits.

29

However the biggest (literally) awe-inspiring thrill is watching the gray whales through our binoculars as they migrate up the coast, continually "spouting off," and catching a sight of their flukes as they breach the waves.

On one of those Scrabblely afternoons, I looked up, after taking my turn, to see a whale particularly close to the shore. It repeatedly leaped out of the water so that almost its entire body was visible. It must have done this twenty or thirty times. The whale seemed to stay in exactly the same place as these joyous leaps went on and for some time. It was as if the whale was just doing it for the sheer pleasure of making a big splash. That leaping leviathan was certainly impressive, but a creature that huge needs some real momentum to get that much "air" under it.

What exactly was going on beneath the waves?

All it took was that question to spark a big leap of imagination, or maybe it was more of a bounce.

Rockets and Balloons

Terry Murdock

I always wanted to work with aircraft and rockets. I made any plastic models of them that I could buy with my allowance when I was a kid. After I graduated from high school, I got my degree in aerospace engineering and was ready to tackle space. One of my first jobs was as a propulsion test engineer for the Mars '75 Lander.

It was an odd-shaped triangular craft about the size of a VW Beetle. It was launched on a Titan rocket and after months of travel, would reach Mars orbit. It then had to deorbit, deploy a parachute, and glide down the final dozen feet using a rocket-braking system. This stationary craft was then supposed to take soil samples in order to look for life.

The Lander was an elaborate collection of propellant tanks, tubing, wiring, and engines designed to set the craft down gently on the surface of Mars. All was going well, and my team was working its way through the propulsion system to make it ready. When it was finally assembled, my boss reminded me that I had to come up with a test to verify that all was working correctly as a system. I had to test it like it was going to fly and steer itself.

The engine pods had small thrusters that fired to keep the craft stable during the descent to Mars, but how to verify that the twelve small engines were firing in the correct sequence?

One night I noticed my young daughter playing with a balloon. Soon the balloon had popped, and she continued to blow on the shredded end piece. As a protective father, I could imagine her inhaling the piece, so I grabbed it away and gave her something safe to play with, like a pot and a spoon. Disaster averted! Then it hit me. She loved the way the shredded balloon fluttered and sputtered when she blew through it. If I could attach a shredded balloon to each of the engines and run a

Viking lander. Source: NASA, https://mars.nasa.gov/mars-exploration/missions/viking-1-2.

low-pressure gas through them, we could see each engine operate.

I cleared this with my boss the next day, and after he had stopped laughing, he made sure that all the engineering disciplines were satisfied with the solution. They were satisfied. I gathered up a collection of balloon sizes and colors and cut the ends off.

Soon we had them attached to each of the engines. We set up cameras to record the balloons fluttering, turned on the low-pressure gas, and fired up the software sequence that sent gas to each of the engines; then we recorded the show. At that point, it was just a matter of verifying that the correct engine balloon fluttered correspondingly to the correct software command. It worked, and we tested three different landers this way. Two of those landers were sent to Mars in 1975 and are still on the surface today. The third is in the Smithsonian National Air and Space Museum.

Sometimes solutions come in the least likely of ways; we just need to recognize them.

Terry Murdock has enjoyed the Fourth of July as his favorite holiday since he got his first pop-bottle rocket. After graduating with a degree in aerospace engineering, he has participated in designing planetary and lunar probes as well as assisting in more than fifty missile launches of some of our country's most versatile satellites.

A (Very) Few Words on Brevity

Leigh Rubin

Too much or not enough? Like in the Goldilocks fairy tale, everything has to be *just* right.

Brevity = no more and no less than the exact amount of whatever is necessary to get the point across. No "fluff," no extras. Just the right amount to achieve maximum impact.

Economical communication—visual, verbal, or written—is a tricky balancing act.

"Man, you really have to admire Teresa. However does she manage to juggle a career *and* a family?!"

Cartoons require a precise balance of art and caption. Too little of either, and you leave readers scratching their heads. Too much, and you run the risk of being overdrawn and under-funny as well as underestimating and insulting the reader's intelligence.

Now I could go on, but....

Baseball and Bikers

Jeff Harman

Back when I was in the sixth grade, I watched a centerfielder, Willie Davis of the Los Angeles Dodgers, play in the World Series. In one of those games, Willie made three errors...in one *inning*. The ultimate in futility, captured on national TV.

Naturally, after the game, Willie was surrounded by reporters shoving their mikes in his face. "Willie, you set a record for errors; how do you feel?" "Can you ever get past this?" "Do you think they'll let you play tomorrow?" and so on.

Now, Willie could have been ashamed, he could have been upset, he could have said, "*Get out of my face!*" But he made a different choice.

Willie just smiled and said, "It ain't my life, it ain't my wife, so why worry?"

What a creative and disarming comeback! Years later, I remembered this lesson of Willie's turning the tables by simply not responding like he was expected to.

That was when I was a CHP officer, cruising the state highways looking for traffic violators. One afternoon, I noticed a biker run a red light, so I decided to pull him over. By this gentleman's appearance and clothing, I deduced that he was a member of a well-known and notorious motorcycle gang.

I informed this rather large individual why I had stopped him, took his driver's license, then walked back to my patrol car to write the ticket.

This guy got off his hog and swaggered back toward me. He leaned back against my car, with that wallet chain scratching my fender, folded his arms, and began to glare at me. Now, I don't know about you, but I just don't like people leaning against my patrol car. So, I said, "Step away from the car."

His noncompliance and facial expression were clear signs that he wanted to brawl with me. Even though I was the guy with the baton and the gun! He seemed quite willing to absorb some pain in order to get some street cred with his running buddies.

Now, even though it is in my job description to "use whatever force necessary to effect an arrest," I had a choice here: We either get to brawlin' and both wind up in the hospital and he goes to jail, or I could just get the job done so we could both get on with our lives.

I looked him right in the eye and said the magic word: "Please."

You should have seen the look on his face. It was *priceless*. He simply did not know what to do...*except* step away from the car.

Jeff Harman is an ex–cab driver, ex-postal worker, ex–CHP Officer, and ex–insurance investigator. He can't hold a job, so he retired to Florida to play softball. In his spare time, Jeff writes short stories for anyone who asks.

Bullet-Sponges and Passwords

Roger Aeschliman

From November 2005 through November 2006, my Kansas Army National Guard battalion was combat-deployed to Iraq. My element ran the theater-wide Joint Visitors' Bureau (JVB) and had the enormous responsibility of receiving, guarding, and escorting dignitaries during their time in Iraq.

This amazing assignment included maintaining and driving a fleet of armored cars, operating a hotel in a palace capable of bunking more than 100 guests, and running a mess hall for our overnight visitors.

Those of us with actual JVB escort duties were directly responsible for the lives of our dignitaries, also known as "packages." If necessary, we were expected to put ourselves between the package and danger; hence we were "bullet-sponges." This was a term we did not share with our wives, children, or parents.

The single most dangerous moment for any mission was the possibility of getting stuck in traffic. There were eight million people in Baghdad, and every one of them owned a car... but not one of them knew how to drive. Traffic jams were a daily occurrence all over the city. Aggressive driving was the norm, and traffic laws were ignored. We were frequently cut off, nudged off the road, or rear-ended by the normal, everyday no-threat Baghdadi. Add in the quotidian Vehicle-Borne Improvised Explosive Device (VBIED) attacks, and our armored-limo convoys were at great risk every time we hit the road.

While our vehicles could withstand random rifle fire or roadside blasts, they could not withstand large caliber weapons or VBIEDS. If we got stuck in traffic, the risk flew through the roof. Hajji the Terrorist could walk right up, slap a magnetic mine on the limo, and blow us away. We bullet-sponges simply could NOT allow a stop in our movement.

While the Kansas JVB was protecting visiting dignitaries, a private contracting firm, Triple Canopy, was guarding the elected Iraqi leadership. With five thousand years of tribalism, differing ethnic groups, divisions between Muslim sects, and a revenge/vendetta culture, Iraqis simply could not trust other Iraqis to keep them alive, so they hired Triple Canopy bodyguards from Central and South America to do the job.

The JVB and Triple Canopy intersected every day. We would deliver dignitaries to opulent palaces in the heart of Baghdad on the Tigris River for meetings with the president, prime minister, cabinet ministers, and military leadership of Iraq. Triple Canopy guards prevented our entry until we cleared their security. It took daily pre-planning to clear this barrier without stopping dead in traffic. We took extra pre-mission time to get to know the Triple Canopy guards so our access would not be delayed.

An additional barrier to entry was that our JVB team spoke little Spanish, and the Triple Canopy guards did not speak English. We would draw pictures, count the number of vehicles on our fingers, and teach each other a few words of one another's language. With this critical pre-planning, we were able to roll through the Triple Canopy barricades and gates without stopping.

One pleasant evening while my package was tête-à-tête with the prime minister, I had a long babbling "chat" with a large number of the Triple Canopy team. In *my* terrible eighth-grade Spanish and *their* terrible MTV-based English, we "talked" about families at home, friends and food we missed, and, especially, girls and beer, which were off-limits to American soldiers (and married Kansas bankers).

In Spanish, girl is chica. Beer is cerveza. We left that night to "Adios, Ash" (me) and "Adios, Juan" (the head guard) and "Donde estan las chicas y la cerveza?"—"Where are the girls and the beer?"

Less than a week later, I had United States Secretary of Defense Donald Rumsfeld in a convoy heading to the prime minister's gates. For whatever reason, the gates did not open, and we were suddenly surrounded in bumper-to-bumper traffic. Since allowing Don Rumsfeld to be blown up would have been considered a career-ending event for a bullet-sponge, I burst out of the limo and frantically sprinted through traffic shouting "Donde estan las chicas y la cerveza?!"

Why great care and consideration should be taken when selecting the proper password

Juan leaned out of his armored gatehouse, saw me, and shouted back: "Hey, Ash! OK. OK. JVB!" opened the gates, and we rolled in with Rumsfeld successfully unblown-up.

On a pleasant evening a few months later, Juan taught me two jokes, one about bull testicles and another about a naked man bending over a bathtub—but neither one translates well into English. For the rest of our tour the secret password between the bullet-sponges and Triple Canopy was: "Donde estan las chicas y la cerveza?" That translates well in any language.

Roger Aeschliman wanted to be a cowboy but shoveled manure, wanted to be an astronaut but puked on carnival rides, so he became a newspaper reporter because no math was required in college to be a journalism major. He's had a great life in newspapers, appointed government jobs, and as a trust officer and especially enjoyed his two, year-long, all-expenses paid, tax-free vacations to the cradle of civilization—where "Yo hablo Espanol."

Diamond Rings and Knuckleheads

Rick Rittenberg

I had just earned a degree in earth science and was applying for geological jobs everywhere I could. But I desperately needed a job "right now" to pay for my upcoming wedding, so I decided to apply for a parts-department position at the Southern Nevada Harley-Davidson dealership not far from where I lived.

On the day of the interview, I met Neil, the tough, no-nonsense owner/manager of the dealership. Neil gave me a tour of the place, starting with the showroom at the front where the shiny new Harleys sat—asking to be bought by anyone who had won a casino jackpot.

The next stop was the shop, where I was introduced to the two mechanics: Red, a crimson-bearded giant Viking of a man who would have looked just as comfortable wielding a Norse battle ax as he would a Craftsman socket wrench, and Spider, a tall, long-haired, lanky guy with web tats running the length of either arm.

The parts department was row upon row of shelves behind a well-worn counter. On the counter were oil-stained parts catalogs with exploded views, which identified the part numbers, of all the motorcycles. On the shelves were thousands of parts, from BB-sized ball bearings to larger items, all organized into bins and sorted by part numbers.

The interview was with Neil and Roger, the slick, fast-talking salesman.

Neil: It says here (looking at my job application) you went to college and rode motorcycles. Tell me about the motorcycles.

Me: Well, I enjoy riding and working on them. I guess I've had a passion for them since I was a teenager.

Roger: What type of bikes have you owned?

Me: Both street and dirt bikes. Over the years I've owned Yamaha, Honda, and Kawasaki.

Roger: No Harleys? Neil, do we need to continue?

At this point I thought I'd be shown the door, so in a desperate attempt to salvage the interview, I tried something else.

Me: Several of my friends own Harleys, and I've ridden them. I really like the sound and torque of the V-twin engine.

Neil: I have a few more questions. What are you riding now?

Me: My last bike was a Kawasaki 900, but I sold it to buy my fiancée's wedding ring...(and then, hoping for a bit a pity), "I'm currently driving a Chevy Vega."

Neil: Do you have anything else to add?

Me: A big part of geology is the study of rocks and minerals. The three rock types—sedimentary, igneous, and metamorphic— are composed of minerals. Minerals are identified and classified by chemical formulas. The formula reveals information about the mineral. For instance, quartz is silicon dioxide. I figure you repair and sell parts for mostly shovelheads, panheads, and maybe some knuckleheads. In the parts catalogs, they are deconstructed into exploded views with index numbers that correspond to specific part numbers. The part number reveals information about the part, such as what year the part was first used. So, mineralogy and Harleyology are very similar.

Neil: Do you have any questions for me?

Me: When do I start?

Neil: Monday at 7 a.m.

**Cool as he was, Rick still needed to
fine-tune his bad-boy image.**

After his stint at Las Vegas Harley-Davidson, **Rick** went on to be a geologist and then an environmental manager. In retirement, he has authored books on muscle cars and mineralogy. Rick's friendship with Leigh dates back to the Jurassic Period, when they were in elementary school together.

Tick-Tocks and Time Clocks

Michael Devine

Long ago in a rodent-centric entertainment company in which I served as a creative consultant, one of the strangest incidents of my working life came to pass.

I was in my workspace, trying to figure out something that would enrich the guest experience while the guest waited in a non-enriching line for admittance into an attraction.

This figuring-out process is known far and wide as "creating" and is not exclusive to folks who think things up in theme parks, but rather is practiced by most everyone who hangs out on our planet. It starts with something in our DNA that compels us to wonder, *"What if...?"* You can fill in the blank from here. In other words, we all have thoughts and inspirations, and when we get them we might act to realize them or file them away (hoard them?) for future development or consign them to the Valley of Nevermind, never to return in their present form.

Back to my work space...a knock at the entrance, and my manager appeared (yes, even free-spirited creative types have managers). She shared the following: "One of the senior executives has asked that I survey the consultants to find out how long it takes for them to get an idea so that he might quantify the time spent."

Well, nimbly side-stepping the impulse to direct that idea to the deepest part of the Valley of Nevermind, I paused. "In my case, a good idea takes thirty-one years (the length of time I'd been designing). A bad idea like that question—there's never enough time."

Like any tale, the moral of this little story is simple: All of us have ideas both good and bad, but it's not a race or a contest. Just take the time to think those ideas over, roll them around, and keep asking, *"What if?"* Those two words are priceless in creating and proofing your ideas and directing them onward and upward—or in directing them toward the well-worn pathway to the Valley of Nevermind. Take your time and enjoy your thoughts; you've earned them.

Mike Devine has spent (or misspent) more than thirty years designing for such household names as Disney, Universal Studios, and others too numerous to mention—so he won't.

Infinite Imagination
MAKING THE COGNITIVE LEAP
Leigh Rubin

When I was a little kid, my dad would often say I was in "my own little cocoon." He was right. While I may have been physically present, I was often away—wrapped up in my own imaginative thoughts. This makes for some awkward moments when, say, my wife is explaining something important to me, and I'm temporarily "out of the office."

We are all blessed with the incredible gift of infinite imagination. We may all see the same things, but it's the *way* we choose to see them that makes everything we see unique to each of us.

One early December day while I was walking my dog, a crow swooped overhead and released a small object. The object fell to the asphalt and cracked open. The object turned out to be a walnut. The clever corvid was using a combination of gravity and the street below as its own personal nutcracker. Having never seen this behavior before, I was curious to see if it was a common occurrence. When searching online, I found numerous examples of nut-cracking crows. That's when the spark of imagination hit. Christmas was just a few weeks away, and with it comes the perennial Christmas favorite, *The Nutcracker*. Suppose a festive crow, deep into the spirit of the season, eliminated the asphalt surface and instead dropped a wooden nutcracker soldier onto the walnut?

Raspberries and Mountains

Margaret Morrison

It began on a hot summer's afternoon as I unpacked a recently purchased box of berries. They were black raspberries—so dark, they were almost black—and expensive. But when I opened their plastic container, I found them so ripe they seemed about to melt into one globular puddle. I thought if I were to quickly plunge them into ice cold water, then drain, they might revive, because that's a technique that works for roses. I probably thought that because the scent when I opened the carton was so richly floral. So after rinsing and laying them carefully out on a paper towel in the fridge, I went to bed, hoping for the best.

When I checked the next morning the berries had become firmer and plumper, though still very fragile, so I carefully removed them from the paper towel, noticing as I did this that there was a roundish "ghost" image on the towel, made by the juice where each had lain. The color was the most brilliant purplish red where each berry's bumps had touched the paper, which then faded outward into a watery pinkish aura. When the last of the berries was removed, I saw an unusual round bouquet-like image, or, rather, the aftereffect of a bouquet—of berries! I knew instantly that I wanted to save it, so took the paper towel into the bathroom and clothespinned it to dry above the tub.

Later that day when I checked the paper towel, I found that the color had not faded in the least through drying. I knew I had to find a way to preserve this exceptional creation because it had happened solely as the result of an ordinary task, and the result seemed so unusual and special. So unexpected. I also knew that with time and exposure to light and the acids in the paper towel the berry colors would undoubtedly fade.

"Fugitive" is the word for this fragile temporary color, and that word also perfectly describes the fleeting, ghost-like quality of the image left behind by the berries.

Now, a little about me: I'm a fine-art photographer and artist and have been creating and exhibiting in solo and group shows for more than forty years. It seems I have an instinct for wanting to document or "keep" things, since that is what I do when photographing still-life arrangements in my home studio. I've explored botanical subjects using traditional black-and-white film and color film, using medium- and large-format cameras. In recent years, I've grown comfortable with the digital printing process through the use of high-resolution scans of my slide transparencies. For instance, one technique I've used to capture minute detail in plants is to place them directly on the scanner glass, later using Photoshop on my computer to reconstruct my arrangements.

It seemed this scanner technique might be the most immediate way of preserving the beauty of this fortunate accident. So I did a few scans, and played around with the digital image from the berry-stained paper towel. As I did so, I was reminded of the look and texture of watercolor paintings. The shape of the "bouquet" as I duplicated it and moved it around on my screen reminded me of the abstracted shapes of mountains or bushes on mountains in Chinese ink paintings. It was this fluctuating impression—Was it flowers or bushes or even hills?—that began to lead me to building *my own* Chinese-aesthetic mountains, but in black raspberry juice rather than black Chinese ink.

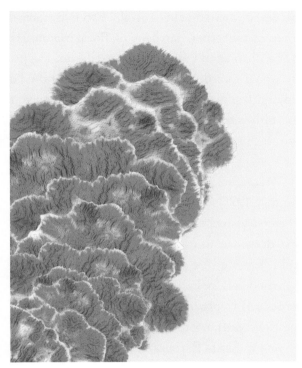

"Black Raspberry Mountain #01," 2014, archival pigment print,
limited edition © Margaret Morrison

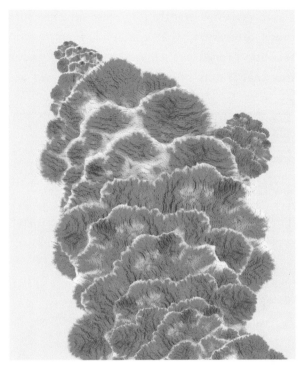

"Black Raspberry Mountain #02," 2014, archival pigment print,
limited edition © Margaret Morrison

It was a few months later, also on a hot summer's afternoon, that I attended an opening reception for an art exhibit in which I displayed the final results of my playful experiment with

Of all the fruit at the stand, the raspberries were undoubtedly the freshest.

the berry-stained paper towel. I had two framed prints of teetering, narrow pink floral mountains in the show...and I won first prize! Later, the juror who'd awarded the prizes asked me how I'd created the pieces; he said he couldn't figure it out, either the process or the material...so I told him this story.

Margaret got involved in photography in the mid-1970s while attending Humboldt State University, in northern California, where she was first drawn to using plants and flowers in black and white still-life photographs. After graduating, she lived in Tokyo and New York City. The gardens of Kyoto, reductivist art, Shinto, and ink painting continue to influence her work. After moving to Santa Barbara, she began using digital techniques, creating forms that can be viewed simultaneously as matter and energy, mimicking in her art the natural processes of growth, decay, and evolution. Throughout, her work reflects her meditation on mortality and timelessness.

Insects and Insomnia

Dave Boito

I had graduated from film school and gone from working as a DHL courier driver (think Fedex but smaller) to working in a "vault." Not the kind of vault where you put money or jewels or gold or silver for safekeeping. This was a vault for treasures of a different sort: film and video-tapes. When an editor of a television show need-ed a film clip, they would call me and I had to dig out whatever footage we had. It was a living. Not the living I wanted to be making. I wanted to be making a living as a writer.

One of the things I did to pursue my dream was write sample scripts for TV shows and sub-mit them to contests. There was one particu-lar contest, sponsored by the Writers Guild of America, which required a script for an existing television show. In this case, it was the half-hour program called *Mad About You*, a sitcom about a husband and wife living in New York City.

As the deadline for the contest approached, I wracked my brain trying to come up with an idea for a plot. Even started writing a couple of the ideas in script form, but they did not work. Dead ends. A good plot requires a good engine. The character has to want something. They have to have a strong goal. What could the goal be?

The apartment I lived in at the time was near the beach. It did not have air conditioning. One never needed air conditioning at the beach, right? Except on one of those rare ninety-degree windless days at the beach. So we were in the midst of a beach heat wave. I lay awake in the dark with the windows wide open, unable to sleep. Trying to think of what this plot would be. No ideas flowed.

Finally, as I drifted off to sleep, a gnat started buzzing in my ear. A really loud gnat with wings that droned as he hovered around my eardrum in the dark. I turned on the lights and swatted it, to no avail. I turned out the lights and tried to go back to sleep. Now wide awake, it took me an eternity to drowse off again. But this evil gnat waited until I was drifting off and buzzed my ear again! I swatted, again to no avail. Nothing like slapping yourself out of a somnolent state.

Several more times this happened. It was as if it did not want me to sleep, as if this was some cruel sleep-deprivation experiment it had designed. Or was the gnat trying to tell me something? I had an idea. What if Paul (the character in the show) were in a similar circumstance? What if a gnat were buzzing in his ear? What if he were trying to kill the gnat, and he woke up from a sound sleep? What if...when he woke up he noticed smoke in the air? What if his apartment were on fire because he left the stove on? What if he were able to put the fire out and save himself and his wife because of that gnat? What if he felt indebted to the gnat and vowed never to kill another gnat in his life? What if his wife insisted he spray pesticides in the house?

I got up and started writing. The ideas flowed and flowed. Goal for the character? Check.

Want for the character? Check. Finished the script in record time. Made the contest deadline. The script, titled "The Gnat," was chosen and acknowledged by the Writers Guild of America as an outstanding freelance spec script for that year.

Things were different before the rigorous volunteer screening process was strictly enforced.

Dave Boito is a novelist and screenwriter. In his spare time, he works as a postproduction supervisor for film and television programs. He can sometimes be seen escaping the screens that consume most of his day—riding his mountain bicycle in the Santa Monica Mountains. He also can be found studying the freezer shelves of his local grocery, looking for new flavors of artisanal ice creams. His debut novel, *Valley Fliers* is available via Amazon and other book retailers.

The Kings and I

Steven Galbraith

Every object preserved in a library, museum, or archive has a story to tell. Librarians, curators, and archivists have the job of revealing these stories in one-on-one consultations, class visits, and even full-scale exhibitions. Interpreting cultural objects for audiences is always a challenge—usually joyful, sometimes even funny. The challenge is determining your story and telling it clearly and succinctly, while also being engaging and, perhaps, even entertaining or inspiring.

I have often thought curating an exhibition was like writing a book. It certainly begins that way. Curators need to research their subjects rather deeply in order to discover the story waiting to be told. The story they discover becomes the overarching idea that is expressed through objects and artifacts displayed in the exhibit. But rather than a book's chapters, paragraphs, sentences, and words, an exhibition's component pieces are graphic and text panels, artifact cases, and shelves or scenes in which the story is illustrated and objects are interpreted. In this way, each exhibition case, each gathering of objects, and each individual object help tell a particular part of the greater story. The sum of all of these mini-narratives is the greater exhibition narrative. To do this, you need to say something about each object that is both educational and engaging, and you need to do it very briefly. Exhibition labels are often as brief as twenty words, and typically no more than one hundred.

For me, the concept of telling a complex story with a minimal number of words and objects was fully realized while I was working on an exhibition at the Folger Shakespeare Library in Washington, DC, about the creation and publication of the King James Bible (1611). My cocurator, Hannibal Hamlin, and I began this story with the earliest English translations of the

Bible (in Old English) and traced translations through the years when English Bible translation was an act of heresy. We then presented various sixteenth-century Bible translations that had preceded and influenced the King James Bible. This, of course, led to the centerpiece of the exhibition—the King James Bible translation itself. From there we explored the vast travels and immeasurable influence of the King James Bible through cultural touchstones as diverse as Milton's *Paradise Lost*, Handel's *Messiah*, Bob Marley's "Small Axe," and R. Crumb's *Book of Genesis*. Printed books, manuscripts, music, and art from our library and those loaned by others dramatically told this story.

But Hannibal and I, along with our exhibition manager, Caryn Lazzuri, thought the story would be most engaging presented through a handful of visual scenes. We imagined a visitor walking into the exhibition hall and beholding the full path of English translations of the Bible before even examining the treasures tucked into the exhibition cases. These are the scenes we chose:

1. A tall wooden stake on which a heretical translator of the Bible would once have been burned.

2. A pulpit from which English translations would have been heard once the practice of translation had been accepted by the English Crown and Church.

3. A household table on which rested candles, a Bible, and spectacles. Reading the English Bible had become a domestic activity.

4. An antique parlor radio. The words of the King James Bible were being broadcast to homes across the United States.

5. An enlarged print of the "Earthrise" photograph taken by Apollo 8 astronauts on December 24, 1968. As they orbited the moon on Christmas Eve, each astronaut took turns reading a King James Bible passage from Genesis on a broadcast that was heard by a half a billion people below on earth.

Looking back now, perhaps Hannibal, Caryn, and I were thinking like cartoonists—telling the greater story of the King James Bible and English Bible translation through five scenes as if they were individual comic panels, or several panels in a comic strip.

Apropos of creative thinking, the one Bible that we weren't able to borrow for the exhibition was the King James Bible used to swear into office both Presidents Lincoln and Obama. That would have been a most compelling artifact to have on display. We couldn't get our hands on a presidential bible, but we did manage to include one king other than James I. I had read about a copy of the King James Bible owned by Elvis Presley, in which, about the time that his mother passed away, he had inscribed "I love you Mama" on the inside back cover. When Caryn called Graceland to inquire about it, she was informed that, although that particular Bible was already on loan to another exhibition, Graceland would be happy to lend another one from Elvis's bedroom!

Long live the Kings!

Steven Galbraith is the curator of the Cary Graphic Arts Collection at Rochester Institute of Technology. For over a quarter of a century, he has spent nearly every weekday in a library and hopes this will continue for another quarter. Rare books are his specialty, particularly those printed on wooden hand presses in the fifteenth and sixteenth centuries.

Moos and Music

Leigh Rubin

Cows are funny. I like cows. I like drawing cows.

Because I have a couple of cartoon-book collections and other assorted items featuring cows, each year—for more than a dozen years now—I attended and exhibited at the annual World Dairy Expo in Madison, Wisconsin. This expo is the place to be if you have anything to do with the dairy industry. It's also the place to be if you enjoy top-notch cheese and/or ice cream. I have made some wonderful friends and business contacts there. A number of agricultural publications publish my cartoons, and I am able to reconnect with the various editors and publishers of these publications during the show.

Selling my cartoon cow books at the expo helps defray my travel, lodging, and booth expenses.

After several years of exhibiting, my booth was getting stale and needed something new, unusual, and bovine-themed to attract show attendees.

One of my sons had recently started working for a small custom-guitar manufacturing company. He was really excited to work there and would share details of his daily work and also describe to me the various steps it took to make an electric guitar. One evening he showed me a

YouTube video the company had posted demon-strating the guitar-making process. I found it fascinating, but what really struck me was how the body of an electric guitar looked to me like the head of a cow—horns and all. I paused the video, grabbed a pencil and a utility-bill envelope that was on my desk, and quickly sketched out a "cow guitar."

Illustration by Leigh Rubin.

This was *it*! A cow guitar would be just the thing to attract people to my booth. Now all I had to do was to have one made.

I asked my son to check with his boss and see if I could visit the company to find out what it would take to have my cow guitar made. A few days later I met with his boss, who is also a gift-ed guitar designer. He really liked my idea and gave me some templates to use in sketching out a more refined version of the concept.

As soon as I got home, I sketched the front of the guitar, but I also had a template for the back. I hadn't given *that* any thought at all, but I started doodling and daydreaming; it occurred to me that if the front of the guitar would be the head of the cow, then the back of the gui-tar would be the backside of the cow—complete with hind legs and tail, but best of all, a big udder.

Now that the design was done, all I had to do was to obtain a blank guitar body, but this was where I ran into my first major hurdle. My son's boss had been an independent luthier, but he had sold his company, along with his expertise, to another firm. Now he was an employee and didn't have the freedom to "gift" me a blank

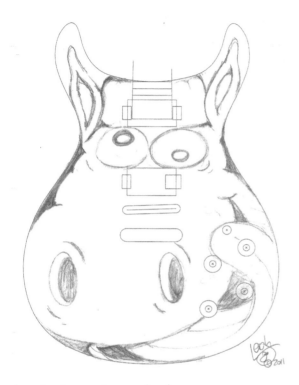
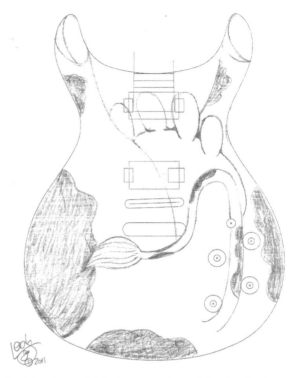

guitar body, so it was back to square one, or at least square two, as now I had a wee bit of guitar-art designing experience.

One of my friends and neighbors, a retired FBI agent and extremely talented musician (how cool is that?!) was in a popular 1960s' cover band, and I remembered a conversation we had had in which he mentioned he had a friend who was the lead designer/engineer of another local high-end guitar and accessories-maker, Ernie Ball. I asked my friend if he might reach out to his friend to see if I could meet with him to discuss the project.

Thanks to my friend, the designer agreed to meet with me, and the outcome was better than I ever could have expected. The company would give me a guitar body to paint, and they would complete the project by clear-coating and assembling it and even provide a case; in exchange, I would paint a second guitar body that they would finish and store in their vault, where their most valuable signature guitar models—those guitars made for such legendary musicians as John Petrucci, Albert Lee and Steve Morse—were stored.

The guitar body I was given had at one time been the signature Music Man® model played by Eddie Van Halen.

As soon as I got home from the meeting, I sketched out the revised front and back designs to fit the new body style, which I renamed "The Moosic Man #1."

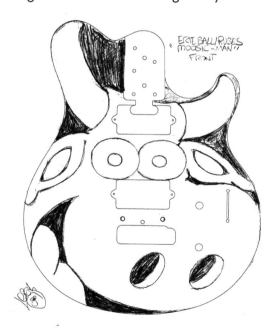

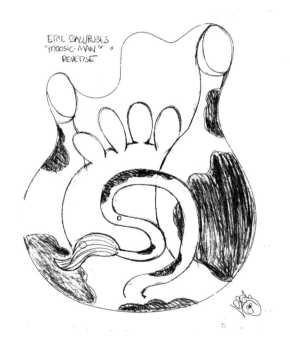

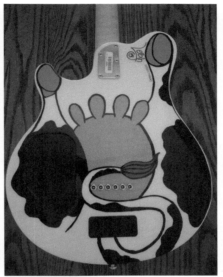
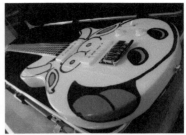

Courtesy of Leigh Rubin.

Of course, sketching in pencil and painting a guitar are two related, but very different, undertakings. But with a bit of practice and lots of helpful advice from their lead designer (aka, and I'm not kidding here, "Director of Geniusity"), my first attempt at guitar painting was a success.

The Cow Guitar, as it came to be known, was a huge hit at the World Dairy Expo. Attendees and fellow exhibitors took turns performing.

Together we made beautiful moosic.

Another downside of hoofs

Lessons from the Spirit World

Deb Goodrich

For a time, I was the resident historian at Historic Topeka Cemetery, *resident* being the operative word. Yes; I lived at the cemetery. It was a dream come true.

When I was a child in the Blue Ridge Mountains of Virginia, Granny took me to the family cemetery, where together we tended the graves, and she shared the life stories of the people who were there—her brother, who died on Christmas Day in World War I; her cousin, who went blind but tended his orchard anyhow; her brother, who built the twig furniture on her front porch. They all had passed away before I was born, yet they were real to me. I understood that their lives were equal to mine. That understanding is essential to the historian, and it is a difficult one to grasp. We tend to view people in the past as different from us somehow, as if they were better, wiser, stronger, more brave. Not so. They were just like us, struggling through life the best they knew how.

When I moved to Kansas many decades later, I became acquainted with the community through the cemetery (because, as one of my friends said, "We're from the South, so we love dead people"). The headstones bore the street names, the building names. I tripped, literally, over the grave of Cyrus K. Holiday, founder of the Atchison, Topeka and Santa Fe Railroad. My fate was sealed at that point: This cemetery would be an important part of my life.

A friend took pictures, and I wrote a little book about this historic burying ground. That gave me the opportunity to speak in front of different groups and become a real part of the community. It also gave me the opportunity to hunt ghosts.

Another friend went into the ghost-tour business and invited me to be part of an investigation in Constitution Hall, a building that dated to our Territorial Period. I jumped at the chance. The crew had placed recorders and some sort of energy detectors throughout the building. I was stationed in the unfinished basement, sitting on the loose dirt, with a very precocious teenager and a newly trained ghostbuster. It was pitch black. Dark. I mean, *really* dark. We sat around a device, some sort of energy detector, on the ground. It looked like a stud finder used by carpenters.

I have to admit, I felt ridiculous.

The ghostbuster began talking. He asked if there were any spirits there and would they please speak to us. He urged the spirits to speak.

"Why would they?" I thought. This conversation has got to be boring them right out of their bedsheets. Even the stud finder was snoozing. If these walls could talk, this place would be screaming at us. The Territorial legislature had met here in the 1850s, and the state legislature in the 1860s. Other rooms were rented to busi-

nesses—shoemakers, watchmakers, spiritualists. *Spiritualists!!!* The man who founded Historic Topeka Cemetery, Dr. Franklin Crane, was a spiritualist. A dentist, he had come to the Kansas Territory with his four grown sons after his wife died. He built the beautiful stone home just east of town on the rolling grounds that would eventually become the cemetery.

"Dr. Crane," I began, "if you're here, I would like to talk to you."

The stud finder was silent, but I kept talking, as if he were standing before me.

"I lead tours to your cemetery, Dr. Crane. They have built a very nice fence around it, and so many good things are happening there."

A faint light appeared on the stud finder.

"I always admired you, Dr. Crane, for joining the Union Army even though you were old (he was 50-something). You knew they needed men with medical knowledge. I know you served honorably through some tough times."

The stud finder lit up.

Every time I talked specifically about his life, it lit up. When I talked about general history, nothing. As I went through the details of his life, a lightbulb went on (in my head; the room was still dark).

"Dr. Crane, did you become a spiritualist after your wife died?"

The stud finder lit up like a Christmas tree.

Did I really talk to Dr. Crane? I have no idea. But if he was there, I was not going to waste his afterlife with small talk and banal conversation.

The opportunity to live in Dr. Crane's former home, now the cemetery office and an upstairs apartment, came a few years later. My adult daughter lived with me, and she slept in the room that was probably his. Each night that summer she pointed the air conditioning unit toward her face and in the middle of the night it was moved toward her feet. After a couple of weeks, she was freaked out.

"Talk to Dr. Crane," I advised.

"You talk to him. You know him. I don't," she replied.

I took my divining rods (a couple of coat hangers I had cut into L-shapes) and ventured to her bedroom.

"Dr. Crane, if you're here, I need to talk to you."

I explained that we were happy to be living in his home and were encouraging interest in the cemetery. In order to accomplish these things, we needed to feel safe, and he needed to help my daughter feel safe.

The divining rods crossed in acknowledgment, and the air conditioner never changed directions again.

Was his spirit there? I have no idea. I am not a medium and profess no supernatural powers beyond those of an investigative journalist and historian. What I do know is people. And people are the same, living or dead. My granny taught me that lesson in a little family cemetery many years ago, and Dr. Crane is just one example of connecting across time.

To summarize, don't let a little thing like death get in the way of making new friends. Granny taught me that.

Deb Goodrich was inspired by watching Lois Lane on Superman and became a newspaper reporter at age fifteen. She has worked in print, radio, and television. In between, she earned a history degree and has appeared as a talking head in numerous documentaries and has written and produced film projects focused on the American West. Generally speaking, she would find you far more interesting if you had died a hundred years ago.

Quarks and Sparks

Michael Kaplan

In 1993, I fled Hollywood, having (barely) survived two writers' strikes while waiting for the city of L.A. to acknowledge my existence and, subsequently, give me permission to leave. Neither of those events happened. So, with my comedy-writing tail between my legs, I slunk off for greener pastures on the Central Coast of California.

I quickly found myself lured to Silicon Valley, where the very first tech bubble was going down. Multiple companies were creating new gaming platforms and software architectures, and everyone wanted to *reinvent storytelling*. That's not a snarky rephrase. I sat through numerous meetings at the headquarters of start-up companies that had just received their first wave of venture capital. The young hotshots in charge would confidently tell my partner and me that they wanted to "reinvent storytelling." We would sit there in some cool conference room, lounging in these $5,000 ergonomically perfect chairs, and nod our heads and assure them we could pull it off. Then we'd go away, hear nothing, never see a contract or a check, and eventually learn that the company had failed to secure a second round of venture capital and was now gone from the face of the earth. But no worry. There was a brand-new startup in its place—with an equally cool conference room and those same $5,000 chairs. They might have been purchased at the previous company's fire sale. I began to realize that the people would vanish, and the software would vanish, but the chairs would endure. If I'd been paying attention, I might have made my fortune in the furniture business. But I digress. This is not a finance story.

My video-director partner and I were hired by Electronic Arts to create an interactive movie called *Psychic Detective*. The concept was straightforward: The main character had psychic abilities and could jump into the head of anyone within proximity and stay there for quite some time, seeing and hearing whatever was going on for that character. So every other person in the story was essentially a camera you could switch to, and like an immersive theater experience, you would end up wandering into different rooms, different parts of the mystery. I announced to anyone who would listen that I was writing a movie that was "thirty minutes long and five hours wide." That became a very popular sound bite, one that got me invited to a few writers' conferences, where I became the poster boy for Oldish Dogs Learning Fairly New Tricks. The Electronic Arts marketing department got downright gleeful, convinced they had a breakthrough hit on their hands.

Spoiler alert: They didn't. *Psychic Detective* was a massive flop. The company never thought about holding a focus group. They might have learned that no gamer really wanted to watch an interactive movie like that. But I digress. This is not a marketing story.

So what does a script look like for a movie that is thirty minutes long and five hours wide?

Well, it's a weird combination of narrative and math, one that required lots of flow charts and short punchy scenes with copious instructions at the bottom of each one about where these modular scenes could conceivably link to next. I was constantly entertaining multiple outcomes for each story fragment and trying to make sure the entire enterprise did not morph into an endless horizon of possibility. And I was losing that battle. I remember one memorable day when twenty-five pages of script and instructions disappeared like a soap bubble from the clunky early 1990s laptop I was working on. The first and (I hope to think) last time I ever cried into my computer. But I really couldn't blame my struggles on the laptop. This was brand-new terrain, and I had no similar models to consult. To put it mildly, I was blocked...and lost in choice.

One evening, in the thick of this struggle, I found myself seated next to Murray Gell-Mann, the Nobel Prize–winning physicist. (That was fun to type. I mean, it's absolutely true—but those were not my typical dinner parties. Normally, I'd be sitting next to Carter, the sarcastic would-be pastry chef.)

Gell-Mann is best known for his theoretical work on elementary particles and, particularly, the development of his quark model. He was also naturally curious about everything and asked me to describe the project I was working on. I began to explain the challenges of the laterally expanding narrative, and he looked truly disturbed. "But how do you keep it from exploding into an infinite number of options?" he demanded to know. I shrugged and told him I was trying to devise little scenes that would behave like funnels—artful, witty funnels—to bring these multiple story strands back down to a manageable number that could eventually multiply again. Gell-Mann broke into a grin. "Ahhhh, it heals itself!"

Somehow, that did the trick. Damned right! My interactive story would repeatedly rupture and then *heal itself*. And with that trope in hand, I returned to the work and barreled toward the end. Sometimes, all you need is the right metaphor to spark the critical breakthrough.

Michael Kaplan has written scripts for film, television, interactive stories, and musical theater. In the early 2000s, he collaborated with Leigh on an animated Biblical soap opera called "All My Chosen People." It is still available for purchase.

Doodling and Daydreaming
(OR, AS I LIKE TO THINK OF IT,
RESEARCH AND DEVELOPMENT)

Leigh Rubin

Raise your hand if a teacher ever called on you when you weren't paying attention because you were either doodling or daydreaming.

...

Oops, sorry, I was raising my hand just then, too!

Daydreaming is often frowned upon, and sometimes with good reason.

In second grade, I was assigned the coveted position of "ball monitor." My weighty responsibility was to make sure all the kick balls were brought out for recess so that my classmates and I could play and allow the teacher to leave the classroom, lock the door, and do whatever mysterious things it was that teachers did when the kids weren't around.

One morning the recess bell rang, and we all ran out of the classroom, eager to play kickball. But in all my absent-minded day-dreaminess, I forgot to bring the kick balls. This did not endear me to either my classmates or the teacher, who, after recess and in front of the entire class, not so subtly pointed out that I was "really in the doghouse."

I can't recall exactly what I said, but I must have mumbled something about it not happening again. Except it did. The very next day—because, you know, perpetual daydreaming. So after being embarrassed, humiliated, and lightly chastised again by my teacher, I was fired.

One online dictionary defines *doodle* as: scribbling absentmindedly.

**"Don't tell me; let me guess. ...
You play outfield?"**

Plus, and let's face it, doodle is just a fun word. It sounds playful, and it rhymes with noodle, poodle, and strudel—things we all like.

Daydream is defined as: a series of pleasant thoughts that distract one's attention from the present. In other words, it's what I get paid to do.

Wow, Leigh, that sounds like a dream job!

Well, sort of. Allow me to explain. Nearly every day for the better part of forty years I have had to create something funny to be published in newspapers, and later, online; something that would feed my family and pay my mortgage. No pressure there, right? Be funny whether you are sick, or your kids are sick, or your dog is sick, or there is some other emergency or family tragedy. Deadlines are deadlines, and they mustn't be missed, no matter what curves life may throw your way. Nope, no pressure there. In other words, "the real world."

Daydreaming and doodling provide a short mental vacation to escape the constant pressures of "the real world."

Both doodling and daydreaming are the purest forms of research and development.

How is that, you say?

Daydreaming allows the imagination to run wild, free, and uninhibited. Doodling is the means by which all that is wild and free and uninhibited is put down on paper.

Both daydreaming and doodling allow for ideas to develop and be refined. But even if an idea doesn't come to fruition, who cares? That's the fun part of R & D; not all the ideas work, so you can just start all over again. If at first you don't succeed, then doodle more!

Of course, you never know where a random thought or doodle will take you. Who knows? It might just take you down an unexpected and creatively inspirational path.

Recently I started out doodling some sketches of pigs and somehow ended up with a gag about hammerhead sharks. Sometimes there's no rhyme or reason to it, but once the seed of an idea takes root and starts to grow, it's time to take control. The random thoughts become less random and, instead, become more organized. That's when the imaginative "dot-connecting" begins to have some meaning and becomes *Directed Daydreaming*.

As usual, instead of paying attention during his most important classes, little Albert Einstein could often be found "doodling" complex mathematical computations.

My advice? Follow your daydreams. You'll never know where they may lead, but you may be pleasantly surprised by journey's end.

Problem-Solving

Leigh Rubin

Have you ever asked yourself any of the following questions?

"Why did the cow jump over the moon?"

"Why did the chicken cross the road?"

Oh, and there's the greatest conundrum of all time: "Which came first, the chicken or the egg?"

(If you haven't, feel free to take a minute or two. There's no rush.)

Now consider the following:

While these questions make for inspiring cartoon material, they may have little relevance when it comes to solving real-world problems.

But they do serve a practical, real-world purpose, if nothing else than as a way to challenge yourself to see how many different ways a problem can be viewed or a situation looked at in order to come up with an optimum solution.

When you have a problem to solve, look at it from as many points of view as possible. The more imaginative you are, the more plentiful are the potentially positive solutions you'll have from which to choose.

Humans love problems. In fact, humans love problems so much that when they don't have a problem to solve they'll often invent one, which, ironically, solves the problem of not having a problem. Problems certainly do make life interesting, don't they? After all, what would life be without challenges? Some people would say it would be a lot easier, but, in fact, it would be just plain boring.

But being stuck on a problem is itself a problem, so try reframing the question.

For example: What motivated the cow to jump over the moon?

Night after night, it beckoned to her. "Jump over me," it seemed to say. ... Now all she had to do was simply achieve an escape velocity of 25,000 miles per hour, and then literary immortality would be all hers.

And what about the second cow to jump over the moon? Why don't we ever hear about her?

The Buzz Aldrin of cows

And suppose the cow's attempt at the "great lunar leap" had been a complete failure?

Now consider these possible fowl-based variations.

"Why didn't the chicken cross the road?"

Or, "Why did the road cross the chicken?"

Why the road crossed the chicken

And instead of wondering, why don't we just ask the chicken?

"Honestly, sir, why I do this isn't such a mystery ... It's a steady paycheck with decent benefits."

But what if we never find out why? Will it always remain a mystery?

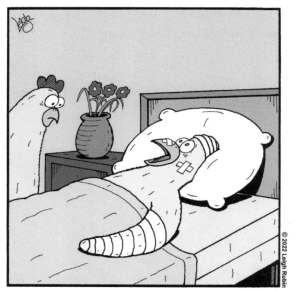

"...And the last thing I was doing was trying to cross the road...But I don't remember why."

Now, assuming both the cow and the chicken know each other, might they have ever compared notes on their accomplishments?

Suddenly, crossing the road didn't seem like such a big deal after all.

. . . and what might the possible outcome be if the chicken and cow ever teamed up?

As far as the proverbial chicken and egg, how was that issue finally resolved?

After a lively debate, it was the larger of the two that presented the most convincing argument as to who came first.

The age-old question at long last put
to rest

The more questions you ask yourself
about the problem, the more inspired and
imaginative your answers will be.

For Mother Goose, inspiration struck at
the most unexpected moments.

Brushes and Busses

Bill Pucciarelli

I have been happily married for the past forty-two years to the same lovely woman. During this time, we have been able to raise five children to adulthood. Although our children, one boy and four girls, continue to make us proud, I would be remiss if I didn't admit to the challenges in trying to parent that many children. My wife and I have been asked many times how we did it, and, I must admit, much of our parenting was a complete mystery. After all, our only model was our parents, and we only had to look back to our teenage years to realize how little our own parents knew about raising children. Our biggest weakness was that we both loved babies. You know, those God-given tiny bundles of joy that you could hold in your arms and who would look at you with unbridled love. If only someone had reminded us that one day, they would turn out to be teenagers.

Being a parent to four teenagers at one time is a hell I would not wish on anyone. There is no end to the challenges that our children presented us. Since I don't have time to list them all, I will address one of the more challenging ones. As any parent knows, getting your children off to school in the morning is very important. If you live in a rural area, as we did, and your children must take a school bus because their school is twenty miles away, getting them to the bus stop on time is imperative.

As most parents know, the school bus waits for no one. Thus, five days every week started with cleaning, dressing, and feeding the oldest four before shoving them out the door in time for them to get to the bus stop before the bus left. Needless to say, if they missed the bus, I would have to drive them to school, and, of course, be late to work. This was something I didn't wish to do, as I had a supervisor who did not have children and was not sympathetic to the plight of those who did.

It did not take long for a central issue to become the overriding challenge of the day—the missing hairbrush. With three girls attempting to get ready in the morning, the lack of a hairbrush would bring the entire morning procedure to a grinding halt. Now what was the problem? As concerned parents, we took meticulous care to see that our children had access to hairbrushes. Yet each morning, nary a brush could be found. Where they ended up is a mystery never to be solved. Perhaps when and if the house is demolished, a hidden trove of hairbrushes will be found.

I have always thought of myself as a problem solver, so I began to look for solutions to this perplexing conundrum. My first attempt was right out of Sociology 101. Buy each of them her own hairbrush and make her responsible for it. Classic, right? Unfortunately, this caused a consequence that I would describe as survival-of-the-fittest or jungle warfare. You see, rather than developing personal responsibility, they quickly learned to take/steal/find someone else's brush.

The first week went something like this: Monday, great morning; everyone had a brush. Tuesday, one brush missing; no one knows where it is. Wednesday, two brushes missing; ditto. Thursday, three brushes missing; only the oldest had a brush. Friday, all brushes missing, but the oldest girl's hair seemed to be combed, although she claimed she didn't have a brush.

Fortunately, I am not one to give up, and I knew there had to be a solution to this problem. I turned now to my more technical side and begged the question: How would a technician handle this? As a fan of Star Trek, I considered a forcefield around the bathroom door that would allow humans to enter and exit but would keep hairbrushes from passing through. Realizing this was beyond my slightly less than scientific mind, I looked for a more practical solution. Surveying my junkpile in the garage, I came across a 5- to 6-foot length of chain for an old swag light. I then drilled a hole in the handle of a new brush I had purchased and attached the chain to it. I also took a sturdy bolt and screwed the other end of the chain to the bottom of the bathroom drawer that was supposed to house our hairbrushes.

From then on, no problem finding a brush in the morning, and at least this problem was solved.

I was recently reminded of this incident when one of my adult daughters was visiting. She now has two teenage daughters of her own and was complaining about the difficulties of raising daughters. It wasn't long before the matter of missing hairbrushes came up. Stopping her, I asked her if she remembered how I solved that problem. She admitted she didn't, and I took great pleasure in relating the story of the chained-down brush. Her face lit up, and she told me that as soon as she got home, she was sending her husband to the hardware store for chain and a sturdy bolt. Thus, my old idea was soon to become a generational solution.

What more could a father ask for?

Bill Pucciarelli is a retired probation officer and parent educator. His best advice to parents is to not lose hope and to wait for their children to grow out of their deviant behaviors. Bill and his wife have been happily married for forty-five years and have five children and twelve grandchildren. In his spare time, Bill is a part-time faculty member at Allan Hancock College and a high-handicap golfer.

Bugs and Nail Files

Debbie May

When the kids in our family were old enough to get our drivers' licenses, my stepdad, who was a master mechanic, taught us how to change a flat tire in the event we needed to if we were not close to home. He showed us where the jack was located, how to put it together, how to find the right spot on the undercarriage to place it, and how to raise the vehicle. He then showed us how to use the lug wrench to remove and replace the nuts on the bolts, making sure we understood that the nuts needed to be tight (righty tighty, lefty loosey) in order for the tire to be secure and not wobbly. The usual maintenance was done by him or one of his mechanics at his repair shop.

When I moved away from home, I had a coworker who worked on his own cars, so when I needed an oil change and couldn't afford to have it done professionally, I would call Steve and take my car to his home, bringing my oil and filter. He taught me about points and plugs and how important a gap gauge is when changing the plugs. Cars were much simpler back then, so I learned how to change my own points and spark plugs. (Who knew this would come in handy some day, actually more than once?) Occasionally I would have to call my friend from home to ask for advice, which became the "Steve's auto repair by phone" joke among our friends.

About a year after I moved away from home, my family moved to the central coast of California, where I would visit a few times a year. On one of these visits in the summer, my brother and sister invited me to go with them the next day to a swimming hole they knew that was about an hour's drive from home. We packed our picnic lunch, and mom reminded us that dinner was at 6 p.m. (as it always had been). My brother, his girlfriend, my sister, and I piled into his little VW "Bug." We played tunes and sang and laughed all the way to the parking area, where they then told me we had to hike and cross the river to get to the swimming spot. Fortunately, the river was not running high, and we had no trouble fording it.

The swimming hole was delightful, and the cold water was soothing on our then sunbaked skin. There were a lot of people there, but the place was huge; we were able to splash and swim as far as we could without bothering any of the other bathers. We ate our lunch and relaxed and cooled off in the water again before starting the hike back to the car. We were tired from the day, so my sister and I dozed off in the back seat while my brother drove, and his girlfriend kept him company.

About half way home, the car came to an abrupt stop—right in the middle of the highway!!! In the middle of nowhere!! In Chinese-fire-drill fashion, we all jumped out and pushed the car onto the wide shoulder. Back in those days, none of us could afford to have an AAA membership, and even if we did, there were no cell phones to use to call for service. Someone remembered a store up the road, but how *far* up

the road we didn't know. And who knew if they had a pay phone there anyway? Ok; we are on our own here.

We then ran all the obvious checks—gas tank half full; starter motor sounded, but would not crank all the way over. OK; now to the rear of the car and open the engine compartment. Yup; spark plugs all present and accounted for. Wires all seem to be attached at both ends. Hmm. My brother got out a screwdriver and removed the points. Yuck. "All crudded up," he said. "Anyone have any other tools?" he asked. I said I might have something. I climbed into the back seat to retrieve my backpack and rummaged around. "What do you have?" they asked. "A wrench? Pliers? A gapping tool?" I emerged from the car holding up my secret weapon!! "Are you crazy?" they said. "A fingernail file?"

With that, I asked my brother to hand me the points. I began filing the crud off the part, revealing enough of a shiny contact space that should appease the ignition gods. He replaced the part in the proper location and asked his girlfriend to turn the key. It tried to start. "Again," he said. She turned the key a second time, and the starter turned over and the engine began to hum. Yippee; we were on our way home once again.

Never underestimate the resourcefulness of your older sister. And, yes, we made it home in time for dinner.

Debbie May is a California native who loves country life, mountains, and animals. Her working life spanned more than four decades, doing administrative work, and, when their schedules allowed, she traveled with her late husband. Now retired, she volunteers for various entities. She loves hiking, reading, genealogy research (sometimes finding a living, breathing relative), geocaching, game nights with friends, and snuggling with her feline buddies, who let her share their home.

Popular mechanics

Jalopies and Bubble Gum

Paull E. Rubin

It was the spring of 1975. I was just shy of my twenty-first birthday and had purchased my first car, a 1963 Dodge 440 with a pushbutton transmission and a very powerful 318 V-8 engine. My girlfriend and I decided to take it out on our first road trip together to Joshua Tree National Monument, in the desert east of Los Angeles. This was during the spring break from our studies at L.A. Pierce College, where we had met. The 440 was a gas-guzzling, beat up ol' brown jalopy with bent-in doors and a trunk that needed a two-by-four to hold it open. I had hacksawed the metal barriers between the back seat and the trunk so we could fit a mattress inside and had decorated it with peacock feathers and paisley sheets to make it look like a rolling art project—at least on the inside.

The trip was beautiful, magnificent forests of Joshua Trees and caves to explore; we were in love with the place. The week went by too quickly, and we headed back home via the Pacific Coast Highway. While cruising through Malibu, I was distracted by a lovely girl on a bicycle, whose hair was so long it was brushing against the spokes. I exclaimed out loud to my girlfriend, "Wow, did you see that girl's hair?" and turned my head around to watch her ride out of view. As I redirected my attention back to the traffic in front of me, I noticed a pristine black Mercedes Benz stopped in front of me. I realized I had no time to stop before rear-ending that very nice automobile. The crunching, grinding, sickening sound of my old wreck plowing into the rear of the Mercedes still echoes in my brain whenever I think about it. I was scared and embarrassed when I showed the very surprised and a bit shocked Chinese gentleman, his wife, and young child—who had all stepped out of his newly "customized" ride—my Identification and proof of insurance. I realized none of them could speak a word of English. I must have looked like a dangerous clown, with my long hair and beard, but I was obviously as shaken up as he was, if not more so. He graciously took down my information and bowed politely, as did I, then I watched him start his car and drive onward. It was only then that I noticed steam pouring out of my car; when I opened up the hood, I discovered I had punctured a hole in the radiator and all the fluid was slowly leaking out onto the pavement.

I had not joined the Automobile Club as of yet, so I was on my own. No cell phones back in those days of old, and I certainly had not nearly enough money in my wallet to pay a tow truck or mechanic. My girlfriend seemed to take it all in stride, not worried much, and casually continued to chew a piece of bubble gum and blow bubbles. At first I found myself getting annoyed at every "pop" that she made while chomping on the bubble. I had a million thoughts going through my head when the fourth or fifth "pop" exploded in my ear like a firecracker. Another thought "popped" into my head. I demanded she immediately spit out the gum into my hand; she had a very puzzled and annoyed look on her face,

but I was emphatic and she complied. I took the gum and plastered it over the hole in the radiator and started the engine. To my surprise the gum held fast, and only a tiny bubble showed at the hole. I knew it would be a race against time, but we high-tailed it through Topanga Canyon and—miraculously—made it to the top, then coasted back down into the San Fernando Valley and somehow made it to her parent's house. I turned off the motor and opened the hood. To my amazement the gum had done the job! A bubble the size of a silver dollar had just burst and the radiator coolant oozed through the puncture onto the pavement until it had emptied its contents. Whew! We had made it! Thinking "outside the bubble," or, perhaps, inside it, had truly saved the day. I had to get a new radiator but was grateful to be back home, both of us in one piece, and my insurance took care of the Mercedes.

New York City–born and Southern California-raised, ASCAP songwriter **Paull E. Rubin** received a Bachelor of Arts from Humboldt State University and following a stint as an archeologist for CalTrans (the state road builders), traded in his trowel and pick for a guitar and fingerpicks, then followed his rock 'n' roll heart across the USA, Canada, and Mexico and throughout Europe. His songs can be heard on radio in many cities across America and worldwide on the internet. He prefers, and receives infinitely more joy from, watching the smiling faces of living, dancing limbs to digging up expired, ancient firedancers. He is also an occasional contributor of sick ideas for brother Leigh Rubin's *Rubes*® cartoon panel.

Alarm Clocks and Desperation

Rodger Nichols

Inspiration can come from desperation, and though it's been forty-five years, I consider a particular example one of my finest hours.

It was the spring of 1974, and I had recently been hired to work weekends at KODL, a radio station in The Dalles, Oregon. We'll get to that, but first some background.

It was not my first job in radio. That had come eight years earlier in 1966, at age seventeen, when the Hood River, Oregon, station KIHR trained me to fill in for DJs who were either sick or on vacation. I had been recommended for the job at the start of my senior year by my high-school principal, Chuck Bowe, because I was president of the Thespians, had appeared in a number of plays, and was taking speech classes.

It was a great place to learn the business. As the only station in the county, the 250-watt AM, known as "The melody aisle on your radio dial," tried to program a little something for everyone. Most of the time, they played what used to be called MOR—"Middle of the Road"—meaning pop rather than rock: Tijuana Brass, Andy Williams, Sinatra, and such. But they also had a polka program on Friday nights, country music on Saturday nights, classical music on Sunday, and a rock-and-roll program on Monday nights. The latter being on a school night, you see, kids would have less chance to be inflamed by the music and stay out late getting into trouble, because they would have to be in early. And evenings featured "dinner music" (mostly strings and piano) from 6 to 7 p.m.

It was a good thing that they trained me, because one morning during spring break, I got a hushed call from the secretary asking me to quickly come into the station. There I discovered that the nighttime DJ, the night before, had gotten drunk on the air. As it happened, no one else on the staff had been listening, but the morning man, when he came in to sign on at 6 a.m., found that the night guy had left half a jug of Gallo Hearty Burgundy behind. Those were the days when the station signed off at 11 p.m., and, in signing the log, Night Guy had been drunk enough that there was a line of 1's trailing off the page.

I started that night and worked six nights a week through the end of the school year and all through the summer before going off to college in the fall. I worked three more summers there, then lived in Eugene, Oregon, after graduation from the university. I got a job making big boards into little boards and installing fences for $1.75 an hour.

One day, while digging postholes in the Willamette Valley mud, rain pouring down my neck, I decided that I really needed to get back into radio—comfortable, warm inside work.

I spent a frustrating amount of time applying to radio stations up and down the Willamette Valley and elsewhere in Oregon. Just before the waiting period expired, when I would become eligible for an unemployment check, I got two job offers—from KEED in Eugene and from KODL in The Dalles. I had since become married, and, unfortunately, both offers were for low-paying weekend jobs, not enough to support us both.

But though KODL was in a much smaller market, it was better suited geographically. By that, I mean that it was only 20 miles from my parents' home in Hood River, and they had generously let us move in with them rent-free. It's a strange feeling to return home to your childhood bedroom with a partner, and despite being grateful for the hospitality, I hoped to make that stay a short one.

I took the job. Fast forward two months. It's Sunday morning, and my job is to sign the station on at 8 a.m. I wake up and glance at the alarm clock, only to discover I forgot to set the alarm. It's five minutes to eight, and I'm twenty miles away. Panicking, I throw on my clothes without shaving, bathing, or eating breakfast; hop in my car; and head east at a rate of speed I hope no patrolman will notice. During the interminable drive, I imagine scenes of the station manager standing in the door when I get there, ready to hand me my license off the wall and fire me on the spot.

It's during this ohmygod-what-am-I-going-to-do moment that I receive one of the greatest inspirations of my life. We always had cats around the house, and I absorbed the lesson from them that if you jump for the top of the end table and miss, sprawling onto the floor, anyone who hears the thump and looks your way will never know your klutzy move because you are walking along casually elegant—as if nothing had ever happened.

By the time I got to the station, I was ready. With relief I saw that there were no cars in the parking lot and that the front door was still locked. Great so far. I headed for the transmitter, kicked it on far more quickly than the manufacturer recommended, then set the needle down in the middle of a record, and when it finished, back-announced three songs. Anyone who had tried to tune the radio in prior, hearing only static, would conclude that the fault was with the radio or some obscure weather phenomenon. Nothing to see here, folks. Just move along.

And it worked. I faked a couple of meter readings that we were required to take in those days, but I believe the statute of limitations protects me from the FCC Police, and the successful strate-gem meant I could hang on long enough to get promoted to full time. I stayed there for more than a dozen years and worked at several other radio stations and for newspapers, but that burst of inspiration I still count today, nearly a half-century later, as one of my finest hours.

The day the worm finally figured out how to beat the system

Rodger Nichols began working in radio at the tender age of seventeen, between the releases of The Beatles' *Revolver* and *Sgt. Pepper*. He later spent a couple of decades in newspapers before returning to the airwaves. For fun, he evaluates coins for estates and writes for a local magazine. In his long career, he has interviewed more than 800 authors, including the editor of this volume, whom he is lucky to count as a friend.

Escape Rooms and Escapades

Juliana Coda

Hello; my name is Juliana, and I am a jobaholic. I typically have no fewer than two, but sometimes I have four employers at once. The problem is, I want to be completely immersed in every experience. (The other problem is filing taxes with six W2s, but it hasn't stopped me yet.) I don't just want to see a play, touch a dolphin, or travel the country. Instead, I have flung open the theatre doors, trained a dolphin to wave, and driven a tour van to the edge of the Grand Canyon. My eternal question is, "Why pay for an experience when I can *get paid* instead?"

That's the *why*, but this story is really about the *how*. How does one apply, interview, and get hired thirty times when they are thirty years old? The answer is by embracing the art of the cover letter. A lot of people assume that a cover letter is a bit of formulaic drudgery, but I never would have gotten this far if I believed that for a second. Writing a cover letter allows you to describe how every event in your life has been leading inexorably toward your getting this position. Writing a good cover letter is exhilarating; even if you never get the job, you got to imagine it and make it real for yourself.

One day I came across a listing for a part time job as host for an escape room. I had always wanted to try escaping from such a room, and, being me, I jumped straight to doing it for work. I knew I was well-qualified for a job involving customer service and special-effects technology. A cover letter wasn't required, but I'm not one to miss an opportunity to write one. I was inspired to embrace the "secret society for protecting magic" theme from the company's website. At the risk of coming across as too "extra" and ruining a fine job prospect, I submitted the cover letter that follows...

Enigma Agent Selection Board:

Included is my résumé for selection as a Game Host agent at Enigma HQ. My prior experiences in theatre and customer service have prepared me to undertake this necessary role.

First, having majored in theatre I am capable of embodying any persona for an extended period of time. My skills of spying and subterfuge will surely allow unprecedented access to the plans of the Labyrinth. Of course these qualities are equally useful in orienting new recruits to the ways of Enigma—pulling back the blindfold to reveal the truth about magic and the centurylong [sic] struggle to control it. It is not unlike my work as a house manager at the Old Globe Theatre in which I orient a team of ushers before each performance and welcome patrons. Let us hope that recruits to Enigma will possess superior problem solving abilities to the theatre goers who cannot locate the restrooms. This is work of global significance, not a trivial entertainment!

Of course I am prepared to assist even the most timid or disorganized groups of recruits through their mission for Enigma. I have extensive training toward that end; I am a level one-certified challenge course facilitator as designated by the Association for Challenge Course Technology. Are there any walls that require scaling at headquarters? No matter, the majority of my 120 hours of training pertains to group facilitation: giving instructions about an initiative, allowing the group to plan, experiment, and fail as necessary, and offering hints or alteration as required to advance participants toward a deeper level of understand [sic] and teamwork. Don't be misled, it's backbreaking work, I assure you.

In fact, you and I both know this is serious work, not all fun and games...at least not for those truly committed to Enigma's mission. I want you to know that you can rely upon me in the most trying of situations. After all, I have learned to handle challenging guests with grace in numerous roles, not least of which as an educator at SeaWorld. I am often obligated to confront difficult individuals and ask them to change their behavior. In these situations I find patience and empathy allow me to assess the situation clearly so that I can offer an alternative solution. While I maintain a relaxed, self-possessed, and polite demeanor, I handle problems firmly and with professionalism. All of this is detailed in my personnel file that was no doubt forwarded by the Committee for Magical Retention, but why I am telling you what you already know?

Over the years I have acquired several more skills that may be relevant to my work for Enigma. I am familiar with your sound manipulation wizardry, having used QLab as a sound board operator and taken a sound design course back in my college days. I am also aware of your visual manipulation software as I have captured images on many covert operations as a photo booth host. Speaking of hosting, a group of like-minded individuals gather weekly at my abode to test their mental prowess at puzzles and games of skill. I can neither confirm nor deny the existence of visual documentation linking me to rogue games of Catan cropping up at weddings across the state.

I hope these details serve to elucidate my qualifications to serve Enigma. Along with my résumé please find a list of witnesses who will swear to every word. I anxiously await notice of the committee's decision in this matter.

Yours in magical cooperation,
Juliana Coda

If you're wondering how it went, I received a reply from the owner that read simply, "Holy crap. Auto-interview. Are you free tomorrow?"

Never underestimate the "mundane" cover letter in effecting results. I've now solved four escape rooms, and I haven't paid for one yet.

Five years ago, **Juliana Coda** dragged the man who would become her husband to Hawai'i with her. She has since held six jobs and currently works as a concierge overseeing the zany requests of the most pampered guests at a luxury resort. Yes, that actually is fun!

"Very impressive resume. You clearly show lots of initiative, but unfortunately, we're looking for someone who can't think for themself."

Ocard and Nagrom

Morgan Young

It was obvious immediately that Draco wasn't your normal, run-of-the-mill child. The first time we met, I asked my new six-year-old student to pick a book off my shelf to read. He then began to scream in opposition when I dared to suggest that Webster's Dictionary was not a "real" book and asked that he instead choose one with a story. Draco falls on the autistic spectrum, with patterned thinking and learning; he tested as being on par with a fifteen-year-old at the ripe old age of seven. Simply put, Draco is brilliant when it comes to math and puzzles, yet struggles in other areas such as social interaction, Language Arts, and communication.

I was placed with Draco as his one-on-one paraeducator. Simply told to "manage" Draco's outbursts. No real training was provided, nor much knowledge on what Autism really meant. Experience and creative thinking would be my only tools. I discovered the only way I'd be able to "manage" Draco's behavior was to discover the root cause of it and find a way in which he could learn to manage in a world very different from his. Every child deserves much more than "management."

On a day-by-day perspective, Draco's biggest struggles included socializing with other students. Picking up on the social norms that come naturally to most of us. Noise and crowds were unbearable because they over-stimulated his mind. The most difficult of Draco's struggles was discovered while trying to build up his social skills. We were very lucky to have a group of four to five peers take a special interest in Draco. With them, I was able to build Draco's skills every day during recess. I soon realized there was a rather large disconnect between Draco and his peers when it came to playing pretend. It made sense to me now, why there was an outburst any time Draco was asked to write about fantasy characters or future narratives, such as an upcoming Thanksgiving break. In a mind such as Draco's, the world may seem very black and white. Things either are or aren't. There are facts in math that hold importance, yet an extreme uselessness in writing or reading anything fictional.

My goal was not only to have Draco understand the concept of pretend, I also wanted him to participate and, with time, enjoy engaging with others in games. This would be a long process. Luckily I had students willing to help. Draco was extraordinarily defiant toward doing anything he wasn't interested in. Once an outburst began to bubble, game over for the day. I would need to tailor this process toward Draco and his needs. His favorite recess activity was skipping. It was stimulating and satisfying for him. That was perfect. I brought some classmates over to skip with him. I created some math activities to do. I found books about bugs and animals and then, with time, was able to convince him why it might be fun to act, for example, like a cheetah. As Draco pointed out, there's no possible way for a human to ever be as fast. He decided to try it. He was loving it!!

Just as the concept of pretending began to take shape, the holidays and with them, winter break, were approaching. The teacher asked the class to write about what they would be doing over Thanksgiving break. This instantly caused an outburst of proportions I had not seen in more than a year. Draco wasn't always capable of clearly explaining what upset him or why. I was finally able to deduce that he found it impossible to write about Thanksgiving break, because Thanksgiving had not yet occurred. To Draco, writing about a future event was like reading a fiction book...useless. So much made sense to me, at that moment. Draco's "random" outbursts toward reading and writing, on days he wanted to do math, weren't based on whether or not he was having a good day. None of his outbursts had ever been random.

It wasn't that Draco didn't have any desire to read fiction or write in hypothetical terms. His lack of desire came from a lack of ability, a lack of comprehension for such things. Yes; the concept of pretending was well on track, but only during recess with peers. The concept of pretend characters and impossible scenarios and the ability to find entertainment in such things didn't exist in Draco's mind. It didn't fit his patterned way of thinking the way math did. Memories of his outbursts when a child or teacher said something funny came back to me. Jokes, sayings, making a play on words usually upset Draco, as he didn't understand what we were talking about.

Some big changes and some new strategies would need to be used. No longer would I allow Draco to borrow a nonfiction book without a fiction book to go with it. While helping him pick a book one week, I, quite literally, stumbled upon a book series called Amelia Bedilia by Herman Parish. These books are about a clumsy, silly, and often confused housemaid, Amelia Bedilia. Each book is filled with idioms, euphemisms, homonyms, and more. Here's a perfect example: Amelia Bedilia was told to strip and wash the bed sheets. So she did. She took some scissors, cut the sheets into strips, and put them in the wash. This was the first laugh Draco had ever made toward a piece of children's fiction.

With these books and Draco's newfound world of pretend, and a lot of explanation prior to reading with him, he was beginning to under-stand why Amelia Bedilia was always finding her way into "sticky" situations—and found them hilarious. Seeing him laugh while reading fiction filled me with joy. Watching him laugh, instead of scream, when the teacher said, "It's raining cats and dogs outside," gave me the final sense of accomplishment in doing what I had been instructed to do. I wasn't just "managing" Draco's outbursts. I was understanding, adjusting to his needs, and preventing outbursts altogether. Draco found his "funny."

I took advantage of this and introduced comic strips, gags, funny cartoons, jokes, riddles. I continued to cater to his interests as much as possible. Draco played the piano, so I showed him my uncle Leigh's (aka creator of this book) series of comedic pictures and jokes all about music notes and lingo. I got him a book of math jokes and riddles. He would approach kids at recess without prompting, which was an absolute miracle and tell them a riddle, revealing the answer before anyone else could, giggling the whole time.

By the end of our third year together, Draco and I had begun to write a short story. Although there were struggles, Draco created two characters and a plot. Math and letter patterns played a big part in bringing his characters to light. He wrote our names, Draco and Morgan, backwards. The unique orange alien, Ocard, and his human friend, Nagrom, were born. Without my needing to think creatively about how to reach Draco, he may never have found his own creativity.

It's been four years since then, and I'm still close to Draco and his family. Prior to writing my experiences, I called Draco and asked him about Ocard and Nagrom. Although he doesn't remember writing a story or the characters, with a little prompting from me and bribery from his parents, he agreed to entertain me. I asked for one activity they might do over the summer. He didn't give me one; he gave me three very detailed scenarios. At the end he said, more to himself than to me, "Ocard and Nagrom would make a good TV series." And they most definitely would.

"Isn't it remarkable what kids can do with a little imagination and a cardboard box?"

Morgan Harman began her career in education at the age of nineteen. Her first job was working at a local high school as a special-education paraeducator, which is a fancy way of saying "teacher's assistant." Being so young, it was sink or swim; she excelled in both. Throughout her twenty years of teaching experience, Morgan has worked with students of all ages, from six to eighteen, favoring high-school level. She is often asked, "Why teenagers? Aren't they a tough age to teach? Isn't their attitude horrid?" The truth is, students exhibit the same behavior at six as they do at seventeen, and the same classroom rules apply: "Stay in your seat. Don't interrupt while the teacher is talking. Stop drawing on your desk. Keep your hands to yourself. Learn to share." In her spare time, Morgan loves to travel, work out, and paint. Teaching keeps her "young at heart."

Fate Ain't What It Used to Be

Steven Hendrickson

Fate just ain't what it used to be. I saw that line in a cartoon somewhere.

Sometimes, cartoons can more succinctly capture a shift in a personal paradigm. Mine was that "follow your bliss" was crap sold by someone raised in a nice family and with the connections to end up safely in the womb of academic tenure and sabbaticals. I, on the other hand, spent much of my childhood in trailer parks, as well as in a chaotic and often violent home. At school, I tried to avoid attention in the back of the room, daydreaming and flunking most of my classes. One teacher concurred with my parents—I would never amount to anything.

So fate, for me, was a job at a turkey-processing plant, pulling necks out of recently slaughtered birds while standing in an assembly (more like a disassembly) line, in blood up to my ankles. I could watch the careworn older workers and guess what I would look like, say, five years, then twenty years down the road.

But I would be proved wonderfully wrong. Side interests would, with luck and hard work, take life down unforeseen alternate paths, which would include a small role in launching a cartoon called *Rubes*®.

It started, only by coincidence, with the passage of Title IX, the federal civil-rights law granting equal opportunity in education. This included giving women the same access as men had to competing in school sports. Area high schools complied by creating a women's basketball league. Getting off work early from the factory, I drove over to watch the first game to show my support. The gym was so empty that no one showed who knew how to operate the gym clock and scoreboard. I thought I might it figure out. I did and would be the operator from then on.

I also noticed that the no-shows included the local media. I had been the sports editor of my high-school paper, but I didn't figure that trailer-park folks regularly landed *jobs* like that. But I dusted off my old typewriter and submitted game stories. One paper regularly printed them. That paper then offered me a paying job as the assistant sports editor.

The pay was low, but I no longer had to wash the turkey blood from my pants after work. The paper was mostly a three-issues-per-week booster organ for local businesses and realtors. It did cover school districts and high-school sports. Spending the rest of my life around high-school jocks held diminishing returns in the rewarding sense, so I asked to be put on the news side. My real interest, however, was writing about music, theater, and art, which I had also dabbled in. The paper didn't see why anyone would want to read about these folks (all productions or concerts here took place in school gyms or banquet rooms), but they agreed to print my stories if I consented to attend and write reviews on my own time.

Problem was, I had no idea *how* to write on these subjects. At a local library, I found magazines covering lighting, stage design, and costuming. I signed up for evening and weekend "writing reviews" extension classes at UCLA and UC Santa Barbara. I visited university bookstores, where I bought books on composition, rhetoric, and criticism. I kept notebooks of reviews I thought particularly pithy, underlining the best parts. And I reached out with a letter to the *Los Angeles Times*' top critic, Dan Sullivan.

To my surprise, he graciously wrote back. And then took me under his wing. He helped me enter a summer writing program, which was under the umbrella of Yale University, in Connecticut, where a panel of critics and editors from the *New York Times*, *LA Times*, *Village Voice*, *San Francisco Chronicle*, and *Chicago Tribune* would shape my meandering, overly verbose writings into something leaner and more focused. And I found myself serving as a literary coach for a play in which future three-time Oscar winner Frances McDormand played Stalin's daughter.

Then more luck, although it may not have seemed so at first. My community newspaper learned that the mighty *LA Times* and *Daily News* were setting up shop in our circulation area. In a staff meeting of glum, already-beaten people, I blurted out: "Great. Let's find out what we are capable of."

We did. The owners opened up the checkbook a little, hiring a bevy of bright, young writers that included William P. Warford. Editors Vern Lawson and Don Hanson supported, as well as unleashed, these Young Turks. We became a daily. And I was able to launch a Friday arts magazine called *Showcase*.

In the midst of this fight for survival, Leigh Rubin paid us a visit. He had been self-publishing clever books with musical-themed humor. I immediately liked Leigh, with his irreverent humor, his endless curiosity about people, and his capacity to find humor everywhere. He would be right at home in our David versus Goliath culture. I asked if he would consider creating a regular cartoon for *Showcase*. *Rubes*® was born.

Here is how it played out: *Rubes*® has been in 400 newspapers around the world, due to Leigh's persistent footwork and creativity. Meanwhile, the Suburban Newspapers of America, in 1987, gave its Best Entertainment Section award to *Showcase*—out of 600 competing newspapers. With *Showcase*'s raised profile for the arts, two area cities built performing-arts centers. The sparkling, outside-of-the-box writing of Mr. Warford and team, wrapped around a real feel for the pulse of our communities, raised circulation numbers and advertising revenue. The *LA Times* and *Daily News* closed their extended operations.

Having discovered that I actually was college material, I earned a bachelor's in psychology from Cal State Northridge. I learned later that the quality of my writing played a major role in my subsequent acceptance into graduate school at the University of Southern California.

My second career was as a licensed clinical social worker, the last eleven years of which was as the director of the Roybal Family Mental Health Center in East Los Angeles. Much of my work would be with teenagers who felt helpless and overwhelmed by circumstance, while flunking out of school and life. But I could sense a spark within them. I shared, strategically, a little of my life and told them I was going to retire and was looking for a replacement.

Their faces would light up. They had just discovered, as I had, that fate wasn't all it was cracked up to be.

Steve Hendrickson, LCSW, worked for nineteen years as a newspaper reporter, columnist, theater critic, and arts and entertainment editor, a career in which he had the honor of publishing the first ever *Rubes®* cartoon by Leigh Rubin, the editor of this volume. He left journalism for a second career as a clinical social worker in the Los Angeles County Department of Mental Health, working with at-risk youth in underserved communities around South-Central Los Angeles. He was director of a children's and family clinic in East Los Angeles when he retired after twenty-five years. His free time is spent searching for new foods, music, art, and (mildly intoxicating) drinks across Europe, South America, parts of North Africa, and Southeast Asia.

Extraterrestrial and Going the Extra Mile

Loretta Sifuentes Genelin

Here are a couple of stories from the licensing of Steven Spielberg's movie *ET, The Extra-Terrestrial.*

First of all, let me explain that Spielberg had recently produced and directed the movie *Jaws.* The licensing/merchandising for this movie literally opened up the licensing industry. It was a smash movie—and a smash producer of merchandising! Before that, licensing was slow and somewhat mediocre. Generally, the licensing rate for all goods was expected to be a 5 percent royalty with a $5,000 royalty advance. The rumor was that this had been set by Disney through its long-established licensing of its characters. Licensing agents at that time rarely diverged from that formula, mostly because licensees (i.e., manufacturers) wouldn't budge very far from it.

Jaws broke that mold. Universal Studios—the owner of *Jaws* licensing—and its licensing arm, headed by Steve Adler, realized the potential of the movie and "went for it!" We broke the then-current records for royalty rates and advances as well as the records for licensing grosses. Everybody was happy! The studio, the licensing manufacturers, and the licensing industry—because we made it possible for them to ask, and get, more for their own licensing efforts on their own projects.

When *ET* came along, nobody was sure it would be a big hit, even though it was a Spielberg movie. After all, many movies that follow a hit often fall flat at the box office or, even if box office is good, licensing might not take off. Nobody knew at that time that Spielberg, though a phenomenal director, would produce hit after hit.

Because of this, possible manufacturers of licensed products were not keen to jump on a bandwagon that might turn out to have no "legs." Also, I was very upset with the scripts that Steve Adler and I had been given because the adorable main character, ET, was killed off (although this, happily, changed later). So, even though it seemed likely that this project would bomb because of the dark ending, Steve and I decided that we had to do our best to license the movie.

In the early script, the main character, Elliott, played so engagingly by the very young Henry Thomas, tries to lure ET to follow him. He doesn't want to scare him away. Reasoning that ET might be hungry and might also like sweets, the same as he did, Elliott takes his cache of M&M's from his pockets and places them in a trail into his house and up the stairs to his room—and ET follows! This is a great scene in the movie.

Steve Adler decided to go after licensing with the manufacturer of M&M's. A natural! Or so we thought. However, the license did not come easily. It was hard to get hold of anyone at the owner of the M&M's brand, Mars Inc. After we finally got a name, it turned out that the man in charge of licensing had gone on vacation—and was unreachable. This didn't phase Steve, a guy who was unstoppable! We finally got a friendly voice at the Mars' offices, and after much cajoling by Steve, a sweet woman told him where the executive was vacationing. We located the phone number, and Steve made the call. More than one, actually.

But the vacationing executive was irate that we were bothering him on vacation and that Steve had the nerve to track him down and call him. Steve explained that M&M's were going to be used in a Spielberg movie and that we expected ("hoped," really) that this movie was going to be a big grosser. That this could expand the sale of M&M's and bring even more profits to his company. Unconvinced, this executive eventually refused to take Steve's calls. (After the movie became a smash, this executive denied ever hearing from Steve, or so it was reported.)

Now we had a big problem, because filming of that segment of the *ET* movie was imminent. And we had to act fast. Production of the movie wasn't going to wait for licensing to catch up. We had to find a substitute product, but there wasn't another such product on the market at that time. But we had to try. So we decided to

126

call The Hershey Company. What a break that was—not only for us, but for Hershey's! It turned out that Hershey's had a new product, Reese's Pieces—directly competitive with M&M's—and were trying to figure out how best to introduce it to the consumer market. We were a godsend for them. They flew out to see us and brought tons of their Reeses product so that we could give them to Spielberg to use in Elliott's scene in the movie.

The rest is history! Along with the movie, Reese's Pieces became a smash hit. The Hershey Company put loads of advertising money into their introduction of Reese's to the market, and, together with the studio's advertising for the movie, Hershey's made a fortune with a very successful rollout of their new product, Reese's Pieces. We were happy, Hershey's was happy, Universal Studios was happy, and Spielberg was happy! Ye-e-a-ah!

* * *

Here's another story about ET licensing and how a different approach to a tough (that's an understatement!) challenge changed the narrative.

All of the ET-licensed products had to be approved by Spielberg's company. The executive in charge of approving licensed products for Spielberg developed a reputation for being not only unreasonable and intimidating, but downright mean! In order to be a kind of pillow between our licensed manufacturers and this executive, Steve Adler took it upon himself to go to every meeting and presentation of licensed products between our licensees and Spielberg's licensing assistant/executive.

Even with Steve's presence at these meetings, this executive was so harsh and negative that many of our licensees were reduced nearly to tears. (I'm not kidding!)

Eventually, the day came when one of our licensees was scheduled to present their products for approval to the Spielberg executive, but Steve Adler was at an important meeting—out of town! I couldn't send our licensee over to Spielberg's alone. I had to fill in for Steve.

Our licensee was a young couple who produced children's pajamas. (They had come in from Chicago, where they had their company.) They were so excited and full of joy at this opportunity that they decided to rent a Rolls-Royce for the ride to Spielberg's offices. Naturally, because of budgetary concerns for this new young company, they had to rent a very old Rolls with a faded paint job and back doors that didn't open. But they loved it!

Since the back doors didn't open, I had to climb into the back seat through an open window—but it was still a glorious Rolls! And huge fun!

When we got to the Spielberg offices, we waited patiently for the exec to make time for us. She finally met us in a small office, where my young couple presented each pajama product and *ET* design to her. Tops, bottoms, and robes with different *ET* artwork, mostly embroidered work, were presented—one at a time. As each was presented, Spielberg's licensing executive would take it up, look at it, and then throw it on the floor—with harsh words of disapproval. She disapproved of each and every pajama product and all of the *ET* artwork used on them.

The young couple were terribly upset. When she threw each of their products on the floor, they were aghast! They would look at her and then at me (obviously hoping I would do something). I let her go through every product. When she was finished, I looked down at the pile of PJs. Since all of her disapprovals were general—"No!" "This is horrible," and similar, I decided to get specific. I picked up each product, one at a time, and asked for specific comment—that is, approvals or disapprovals—on art lines and shapes; the color of ET; his eyes, which were very special; and all aspects of the *ET* artwork—so that at least my licensee could limit changes, if any, to something definite. I did this with every single item. It was surprising how little we actually would have to change by the time we finished.

As we got to the end of the products, Mr. Spielberg himself came into the room. We showed him the children's PJs, and he absolutely loved them and the *ET* artwork. They were approved! (His licensing exec didn't look too happy.)

We rode triumphantly in the old Rolls back to Universal Studios.

Their PJ products were such a success that, according to the father of one of them, they were able to buy their first home.

Loretta Genelin (nee Ayala, Sifuentes) was born in LA (that's Los Angeles) so long ago you could actually see the mountains to the north when you stood on Broadway in downtown. She went to high school in LA (St. Agnes, also in downtown) and then to UCLA, where she got her BA and then her JD (that's LAwyer). After that, she worked at Universal Studios for several years, where she saved her boss from many *ET* mishaps. But mostly, they had fun. Loretta loves LA!

News and Neighbors

Valerie Vaz

When you manage an advertising department for a small local newspaper, at times you need to wear multiple hats.

While I was working late one evening, my office telephone began to ring. It was rare for someone to call after hours, but I answered it. The caller—I will call him Sam—somewhat surprised to get a live person versus voicemail, proceeded to give me an earful about missed deliveries of his daily newspaper. By the escalation in his voice, I had a feeling this was not a first-time occurrence. Sam continued to explain that several days were missed that week. He explained that he relied on our circulation team to deliver his local newspaper and the *Wall Street Journal*. According to Sam, the neighborhood carrier had recently moved out of the area. A-ha! A clue. I continued to listen to Sam and assured him that I would elevate his complaint to the circulation manager first thing in the morning. I requested

the basic information: name on the account, address, the date the issue began, and how many days were missed. Sam seemed highly skeptical of my abilities to solve his issue. OK; I will give him that. As a messenger, could I really make sure he received his morning newspaper? As I wrote Sam's address, I smiled, realizing that it was the same street where I had lived temporarily when I first moved to town. It was one of those neighborhoods that held summer block parties, and neighbors looked out for one another. In my short (five weeks) stay, I had been included in one of those very parties. I decided that it would be a quick drive to deliver the newspapers to Sam on my way home that evening.

I rummaged through stacks of newspapers in the dark warehouse to locate each newspaper. I drove the ten minutes to Sam's home. Not wanting to disturb him, I placed the newspapers on his doorstep along with my business card and a note of apology. As I returned to my car, I could see someone waving at me from the kitchen window across the street. It was my friend, to whom I will refer as Linda, who quickly came to the door and invited me in for a glass of wine. "Sure," I said. It would be a nice way to end my day. Being a good, and curious, neighbor, Linda asked what I was doing at her neighbor's house. I shared that we had recently experienced circulation challenges in her neighborhood. She said, "Yes, I know; it has been the talk of the neighborhood. In fact, I am the one who gave Sam your number." We both had a good laugh and returned to our wine.

We caught up over the next hour until interrupted by a knock on her front door. Standing in the entryway was a man who had just returned from a run. Smiling, he proceeded to thank Linda and shared, surprisingly, "You will never believe this, but your friend personally delivered my newspapers this evening! Can you please thank her for me?" Linda asked, "Would you like to thank her yourself? She is here right now." As Sam entered the dining room, I stood, smiled, and introduced myself. He responded, grinning ear to ear, "Can I give you a hug?"

Sometimes, a little extra goes a long way.

Valerie Vaz had a newspaper career that spanned two decades across multiple California communities. Eventually, it led her to the beautiful Central Coast. With a passion for marketing and helping businesses grow, Val also enjoys community service. She holds board positions with the San Luis Obispo Chamber of Commerce, SLO County YMCA and the Land Conservancy of SLO County and is a regular volunteer with Arroyo Grande in Bloom. For fun, Val enjoys gardening, travel, and spending time with friends and family.

Patches and Pandemics

Leigh Rubin

A hundred years ago, give or take fifty, I was a Boy Scout. Never made it to the Eagle; Star was as far as I got. It always felt like a goal never completed, a job left undone.

A few years back, Karen, a scouting mom and friend, asked me to design a patch for her son's Boy Scout troop. Patches are actively collected and traded in the scouting community. The patch would be sold in a fundraiser to cover the cost of various scouting activities.

Previous patch fundraisers included designs featuring characters from Charles Schulz's *Peanuts*®, Jeff Kinney's *Diary of a Wimpy Kid*, and Hanna-Barbera's *The Flintstones*. It would be an honor to be among such impressive company.

Though my time to achieve Eagle Scout had long passed, there would be satisfaction in knowing my patch—in some small way—would support Scouts working their way toward becoming an Eagle.

The objective was to dream up something fun, silly, and appealing that would also be "on-brand" for Scouting.

The first thing that comes to mind is the uniform, complete with classic "Smokey Bear" hat and neckerchief, as well as hiking and

campouts—"the great outdoors." And, of course, wildlife.

Looking back for inspiration to all the many wildlife cartoons I'd drawn over the years, one especially silly gag had been popular on greeting cards and, later, social media: two bunnies posing for a photo being taken by a third. One bunny, unbeknownst to the other, was giving the second bunny "rabbit ears."

Borrowing liberally, I replaced two scouts for the bunnies—one snapping the photo as the other was smartly saluting for the camera. Instead of a third Scout, a grinning bear pops out from behind a tree, giving rabbit ears to the posing Scout.

Karen loved the cartoon patch and submitted it for approval. Months went by, and despite numerous follow-ups, first by Karen and then by me, for reasons that remain a frustrating mystery, the patch was never commissioned.

I thought about the patch from time to time, occasionally reaching out to Scout-affiliated friends, offering them the art free of charge. No takers. Until I called Thom, a Rochester, New York, friend who once served on the board of the

local Boy Scout Council for several years. Thom set up a meeting with them for fall 2019.

The meeting was delightful, and over the next few months we stayed in touch, brainstorming on the best way to use the patch for a fundraiser.

Then, just a few months after our meeting, along came the COVID-19 pandemic. Most of the country, most of the entire world, went into shelter-in-place, quarantine, or lockdown mode, putting the kibosh on public gatherings, including Scouting activities. No troop meetings, campouts, or any other get-together.

One morning in March 2020, my contact at the council called with a fundraising idea: Would I design a patch incorporating virtual camping, social distancing, and Scouting?

The Boy Scout motto is "Be Prepared," so when I was told the design for the patch would have to be done in just a few days, I was prepared to drop everything else I was working on to get the job done. Publication of the council's newsletter announcing the fundraiser was imminent.

Nothing like a tight deadline to get the creative juices flowing.

Camping means campfires.

Campfires mean marshmallow roasts.

Marshmallow roasts require long sticks.

Virtual means laptop.

Social distancing means apart.

How about roasting virtual marshmallows on a virtual campfire while maintaining a proper social distance?

The initial design was submitted within a couple of hours.

SOCIAL DISTANCING
PATCH/MERIT BADGE
CONCEPT SKETCH

The folks at the council were pleased, and the design was approved. The fundraising campaign kicked off and was a big success, with more than 1,200 patches sold. The money raised was used to fund the tech support necessary to transition the 8,000 Seneca Waterways Scouts from in-person to virtual activities and events.

Oh, and the original art with the bunnies? The Boy Scouts sold signed prints for another fundraiser.

All it took was being persistent long enough to find the right contacts willing to make my patch idea a reality—and being prepared to meet a stiff deadline...Scout's honor.

One and a Multitude

Lorraine Payette

In the modern world of small-town weekly newspapers, editors come in all shapes, sizes, and temperaments. Most of them are young and under-experienced, hired straight out of school and put into positions of power that are overwhelming to them. For many, the system is like a revolving door—with them in the big chair one day and out again soon after, while some of them are determined to stick it out no matter what.

Each editor du jour has a personal way of wanting things done. Sometimes something is short, sweet, and simple, needing little more than a photograph to cover it; other times you may need a series of articles in order to make it work. Experienced editors will know instinctively which is which and will make sure that things are handled accordingly. The inexperienced have a lot more trouble with these judgment calls. As a journalist, your job is to make sure the news gets out properly, in spite of any peccadilloes that might come along.

One eager young editor was bound and determined to claw her way to the top, no matter what. Unfortunately, she was unable to understand flexibility or the need to view each case independently.

Someone had told her that because rural weeklies were very small, with small readerships, they shouldn't devote more than one article to any one topic. And she stuck firmly to that idea—no one, no matter who or what they were—would ever be allowed more than one article. You could have a promotional article saying that an event was in the offing, or build up the development of that event, or do an invitation telling people when and where to attend the event, or cover the event, or do a follow-up and thank everyone involved. However, you couldn't do all of these—only one.

In one village, members of the local Legion and Historical Society had a wonderful vision. They had no war memorial, no way to honor the local men and women who had given their lives in service to their country. They convinced the community of the need for such a memorial, then applied for numerous grants and donations in order to make the vision a reality. I, as a member of the press, was called to come out and help cover this massive project.

The first article got through—the funding had come together, and materials had been purchased or donated to start building the memorial. Stones and arches were put into place, a flagpole installed, plaques listing the names of the honored dead purchased and engraved. Volunteers came out to put the whole thing together.

The second article was picked up by a different paper, but under the same syndicate. This time, the search was on to find family members of all of the veterans and war dead and to make sure their stories would be heard and recorded. These materials were vitally important to the project, and the family members were asked to please send them in to share.

The time of dedication was at hand, but three (articles) was not to be the charm. Politicians from federal to municipal governments would be there. The Armed Forces had been invited, as had Legionnaires from throughout the region and all of the family members who had been so carefully sought and found. This would be enormous. They needed every level of the press and an audience of all ages.

Although written as the all-important invitation designed to bring out the crowds and multiple levels of the media, the editor said, "No." There was no way she was going to allow any more space to be wasted on this. Move on or find work at another paper.

Things were not going well, but people in media tend to know other people in media. The article had been written; it was ready to go, so I tucked it into an email to all of my friends in the industry with a simple note explaining that my editor refused to print it. I told them I didn't expect them to pick it up, but I would be delighted if they would do their thing for the good of the community.

Local radio ran free ads announcing the event. Television wasn't going to be outdone and sent their people over to interview the head of the project. On the day of the celebration itself, press had come in from the nation's capital as well as from throughout the province—radio, television, print—no one wanted to miss this. The crowds came out in multitudes, spilling into the street to get their chance to be part of such an important occasion.

When it was over, I wrote a quick note to my editor. I explained to her that I had followed orders and would not be sending her an article about the dedication, but I was sure that several of the other papers in the syndicate would be happy to share something with her if she wished. In this way, I was able to make sure the memorial and all involved got the coverage they needed while I still managed to stay within the rules.

Courtesy of Lorraine Payette.

Just in case the water failed to part, there was always a workaround.

Lorraine Payette is a multimedia Pollyanna journalist, hailing from Canada, who grew up wanting to be a veterinarian, or maybe an architect, or possibly she would tap dance through life as a glittery unicorn butterfly. She looks for the positive in every situation, and if it can't be positive, she'll try for the funny every time. She plans to spend her retirement...Wait a minute, what *is* retirement? And will there be cake?

Rain and Roses

Julia Shaw

It was spring 2010. My relationship with my boyfriend had expired with our apartment lease. I packed up the computer and the dog and moved back in with my mom. I was down, but not out. In fact, I decided it was time for me to move out of Los Angeles and in with my best friend, who had preceded me to Portland, Oregon.

So, I sold most of my stuff, crammed as much as I could into my compact car, and went road tripping with my Bichon Frise mix. Now, I had only been to Portland once, but had visited family in the Pacific Northwest for years. And, frankly, I *hated* it. I did not like the cold, the gloom, or—God forbid—any wet weather.

My dog has always fit with my personality—happy-go-lucky, but with an aversion to rain. In fact, we had a routine for walking in the rain. I would coax him to go to the bathroom, and as soon as he did his business, I'd pick him up, shove him under my jacket, and sprint for the door. He learned to take very quick potty breaks during the infrequent rainstorms we experience in Southern California. He didn't even like sprinklers.

All of this is to say that I made my move more out of a deep desire for change than because I love the Pacific Northwest.

I could go on for pages about my journey up through San Francisco and the sweet seaside town of Trinidad, to the one-street village of Garberville, where I stayed in the only motel-cum-apartment complex and ate at the only restaurant in town. My trip took me through the extremely conservative berg of Bandon (a sweet old lady asked me why I'd want to go to Portland, with all those "crazy liberals," after spending thirty minutes complaining about Bandon's meth problem) and, finally, to my friend's apartment in Portland.

I settled in with my bestie and her boyfriend, getting on the lease and sharing the rent. My friend, Amy, set me up on my first blind dates ever. They were all terrible, with one dude telling me he was moving to Idaho the next day. On top of the miserable dating scene, it was freezing (to me, a Southern-California native), and I hadn't seen the sun— or even the moon—for over a month. I called my dad and told him I wanted to get the heck out of this horrible, depressing, sunless place.

Then I met the cute accountant at work. We worked in a tiny company, and his mom—a friend of Amy's—had gotten him the job. Amy, in turn, had gotten me a job. So, we were all loosely connected. But Ryan was a quiet guy. He didn't talk with anyone, just came in, did his job, and left. His strong and silent act reeled me in, and I wanted to find out what his deal was.

Part of my job was pulling various court records, which often cannot be done online. So, I visited local courthouses fairly often. One day, I was going downtown to pick up some records and, since the day was just about over and Ryan took the bus, I asked if he wanted a ride down-

town. He said yes and gathered his stuff and left with me. The car ride was absolutely silent. I tried to get him to play music he liked or tell me about himself or talk about the best spots in the city or *something*. Nothing.

Finally, he told me I could pull over and drop him off at the park in front of the courthouse. He held the door for a moment and then said: "Do you like coffee?" I replied in the affirmative. "Good, then go get some at Stumptown. Do you like donuts?" I was on a diet and told him so. He rolled his eyes. "Go to Voodoo Donuts." Then he slammed the door.

I rolled my eyes and found a parking spot, getting on with my work. But that weekend I went to Stumptown and Voodoo and tried the coffee and donuts. I was actually a bit of a coffee snob (still am), and Stumptown was good.

The next Monday, I told Ryan what I'd done and asked where else I should check out in Portland. He recommended I read Chuck Palahniuk's guidebook and then, once again, he clammed up. That sparked an idea. If I was going to get this cute boy to talk, I was going to use my limited knowledge about his interests and force him to open up to me.

So, every day I would read guidebooks about Portland, and every day I would pull questions to which I already knew the answers from the books. I would ask him things like "Oh, I want to visit every bridge in the city—what's that big red one?" or "When do the cherry blossoms bloom downtown? I'd love to see them," or "What's that white fluff floating in the air?" or "This book says I should see the International Rose Test Garden; what do you think?"

My badgering him about his favorite topic—his hometown—got him to open up. And that question about the Rose Garden? Well, he told me that I should see it—with him. We had our first date up there and got married in Washington Park, which is positioned just below that lovely place.

Ten years later, I have learned to love Rose City—with cloudy, but glorious, springs and brisk, but vibrant, autumns. I still kind of hate winter, but I have made a warm home with my husband of eleven years, our dog (who no longer minds the rain), and our sweet daughter.

"Sorry, lady, not having enough time is no excuse. Next time I catch you for failing to stop *and* smell, I'm going to have to cite you for committing a fragrant violation."

Julia Shaw is a copywriter and author. She lives in Portland, Oregon, with her small child, husband, and elderly dog. For fun, she takes far too many pictures of her child and dog, gardens, bakes, reads, and explores the local beaches.

Media and Microbes

Jay Hardy

First of all, you need to know that our company, currently consisting of roughly 440 workers, manufactures culture media that microbiologists use in the laboratory. Culture media is what we call the "bug food" that bacteria and fungi feast upon. The culture results help microbiologists identity the pathogen and also aid in determining how to kill it in order to restore the health of the patient.

The year was 1980, and I had just finished a one-year internship at a hospital in Santa Barbara, training as a medical technologist. These are people who are licensed to conduct laboratory tests in a clinical setting. The requirements are a bachelor's degree and a rigorous year of practical training in the hospital lab. After finishing and passing the California State Board exams, my dream had been realized; I had finally become full-fledged medical technologist.

However, there were no jobs available at the time! Having come from the LA area, spending a year on the Central Coast of California was like paradise to me, so I very much wanted to stay in Santa Barbara. Disappointed and dejected about not being able to find work in my new profession, I was talking to my friend who had also completed the internship. We did not know which way to turn, but somehow came up with the idea of making culture media. My father was an entrepreneurial pharmacist who had operated many drugstores during his career, so starting a new business seemed to be a somewhat natural path for me.

My friend and I started our fledgling business on a shoestring budget. We rented two small rooms in what had once been a motel in Santa Barbara. After borrowing $10,000 from each of our dads and rescuing some antiquated equipment from a trash heap, our little business was ready to be launched. We started with one customer, which was the hospital where we had trained. Over the years, we began to service more and more hospitals in Central California, and we eventually grew into a company that now supplies more than 10,000 laboratory customers worldwide, with over 13,000 products that are used in the laboratory.

I often stop and wonder how different my life would have been if I had gotten my wish and had been offered a job back in 1980. When faced with adversity, I am constantly reminded of one of my favorite sayings, which is the Marines' motto: "Adapt, Improvise, Overcome." We did just that, and I'm now enjoying the ride—with no regrets!

Being both the son and grandson of serial entrepreneurial pharmacists, **Jay Hardy** learned business best practices at a very early age. After achieving a degree in biology, Jay took a more practical approach by interning in medical technology at a large hospital in Santa Barbara, California. Desiring to get into business for himself, he started Hardy Diagnostics in 1980 with a fellow student. On a shoestring budget, they rented a converted motel room in Santa Barbara. The company, which manufactures medical devices and culture media for laboratories, has now grown to about 440 employees. Ten years ago, Jay spread the joy of business ownership by selling his shares to the workers, so it is now 100 percent owned by the employees.

Plutonium and Potpourri

Rick Brown

In the 1980s, my company, Rustic Woods, purchased empty seed cones from companies in California and the Pacific Northwest. These cones were collected for their seed stock and ground up for garden mulch. But we developed a market for what once was waste by recognizing its potential value to manufacturers in the emerging potpourri-blends industry.

Before long, we were shipping truckloads of empty cones to clients all across the country.

In mid-spring of 1986, my largest customer, Aromatic Industries, called and told me they no longer needed my cones due to the April 26, 1986, Chernobyl nuclear disaster, which destroyed all the flower crops in Eastern Europe. If the flowers they used in their potpourri products didn't exist anymore, then they would no longer have a need for my pinecones. Losing them as a customer would effectively put me out of business.

Yikes! What to do next?

I had to come up with an idea—and fast.

What if it were possible to mimic Mother Nature?

I approached the founder of a local landscape and garden-products supplier and manufacturer in Eugene and asked him if he thought it was possible to dye wood shavings to simulate the type of flowers that were no longer available from Europe. The founder was a tinkerer by nature and was all for the idea. He had started his business by collecting and cleaning all the wood waste and shavings from local wood mills and turning this waste into garden-mulch products. It was a natural fit.

The founder agreed that he would build a plant to manufacture my "flower chips" if I could provide him with enough volume to make it worth his while, but, of course, I would have to make the samples first.

I spent the next three days in my basement (and in my underwear), covered in bits of wood like some sort of mad scientist, experimenting with various ways of dyeing and drying shavings so they would replicate the flowers that were wiped out in Europe. And it worked!

The next step was to call to Aromatic Industries and tell them I had a solution to the flower shortage. I asked to set up a meeting with them so I could pitch my sample "flower chips" in person. Just a few days later, I flew down to Southern California with samples of my product in hand.

These efforts paid off, as they were wowed by my presentation and samples. They wanted to order my product immediately, so I pulled a number out of thin air and told them that in order to build this plant I would need a purchase order of 360,000 pounds at $1.25 per pound, for a total of $450,000—and they agreed!

I took the purchase order to my bank in Eugene, and together with the local landscape-product supplier, they made a deal to set up a plant to dye, dry, pack, and ship colored wood shavings to Aromatic Industries. The plant worked seven days a week, twenty-four hours a day for two years until the flower crops recovered in Eastern Europe.

The desperation of losing my best customer was the fuel for this innovative solution. Unforeseen disasters like Chernobyl and challenges such as losing your income become forced opportunities for entrepreneurs to pivot, innovate, and shine. It takes a tough skin, logic, humor, and the guts to get back up on your feet once you've been knocked down.

I believe people create their own opportunities, but, certainly, timing and world events over which we have no control cannot be overlooked. Sometimes I reflect that my birthday of April 26 is the same day as the Chernobyl nuclear disaster.

Rick Brown was raised in Brooklyn New York, attended college in California, and since the mid-1970s has lived with his wife, Lynda, in Eugene, Oregon. Currently a small business owner, he co-operates "Laurel Hill," an online fiber-arts business, with his son Daniel, a PhD candidate at the University of Oregon. A lifelong entrepreneur specializing in start-up projects, Rick now considers himself semi-retired, working "Laurel Hill" and helping his wife manage and maintain family real-estate and stock-market investments. Hobbies include walking, swimming, gardening, and simply enjoying nature.

Serious Business and Funny Business

Rick Newcombe

Imagine being thirty-four years old and running the third-largest newspaper syndication company in the world and working with cartoonists who had created some of the most successful comic strips in history, such as *Dennis the Menace, Wizard of Id, B.C., Steve Canyon, Mary Worth*, and *Momma*.

That was me—traveling the world by flying first class, staying at five-star luxury hotels, and dining at some of the finest restaurants on the planet as well as having a huge staff and enormous company resources at my disposal whenever I needed something.

Then, out of the blue, the company was sold, and I was suddenly out of a job.

I was thirty-six at the time, married and with two children, a mortgage, and a whopping $900 in my bank account, which was my total net worth. I didn't even own a car. I had been driving a company car, and on the day I left the office for the last time, I drove home and went for a run to clear my head. When I returned, my wife was fighting back tears. She said that two big guys had just come to the house to take back the company car. She was standing there with our two children, ages seven and four, watching them drive off with what had been our primary means of transportation.

How do you connect the dots when you can't even see straight?

Well, I calmed down and thought about what I had learned in fourteen years in the business world. I had become an expert in comic strips and cartoons, and I knew that I could always make a living syndicating them. But I also knew that I did not want to be so vulnerable again, which meant that I wanted to start my own syndicate, and I knew it would have to be different.

That's when I thought about the one issue the majority of cartoonists were complaining about: Who should own the cartoon, the syndicate or the cartoonist? At the time, the answer was the syndicate.

When I first met the legendary Milton Caniff, we had lunch in New York, and he told me about his career. During the 1940s he had created the most popular comic strip in the country at the time, *Terry and the Pirates,* featuring the famous Dragon Lady character. He said that since he had created this comic strip, he thought it was only fair that he own it, but his syndicate said, in effect, "Tough luck. We own it." He felt so strongly about the issue that he walked away and created a whole new comic called *Steve Canyon*, but only on the condition that he be allowed to own it, which he was.

Hank Ketcham told me that he had been "hog-tied" by his syndicate ever since he created *Dennis the Menace*. He had filed a lawsuit against his syndicate in the 1960s, and he lost.

Johnny Hart, creator of *B.C.* and *Wizard of Id*, said that he had secured ownership of his two strips, and he encouraged me to start the first syndicate granting ownership to cartoonists. Same with Mell Lazarus, creator of *Momma* and *Miss Peach*. They said that if I started such a syndicate, they would eagerly join as soon as their contracts allowed.

So I started researching this issue and discovered that it went back to the beginning of cartoons in newspapers.

I learned that the very first comic strips increased newspaper readership dramatically. The Yellow Kid was a character in Richard Outcault's comic strip, *Hogan's Alley*, which ran from 1895 to 1898 in the *New York World*, which was owned by Joseph Pulitzer. But William Randolph Hearst owned *New York Journal*, and he was determined to win the circulation war with Pulitzer, so he hired Outcault and ran the Yellow Kid on the front page. Hence, we got the term "yellow journalism." (Also, I suspect that the presses in those days occasionally bled yellow all over the page.)

In fact, cartoons were so good for business that Hearst decided it was not enough to run them or sell them to other newspapers; he needed to *own* them, and this became a mandate for the syndication company he founded in 1914, King Features Syndicate.

One of his most successful comic strips was *The Katzenjammer Kids* by Rudolph Dirks, which started in 1897 and was syndicated by King Features. At some point, Dirks asked Hearst for ownership of his creation, but Hearst said no. So Dirks filed a lawsuit—and lost.

Nothing had changed since then. As a budding entrepreneur, I knew that if Creators Syndicate were the first in history to grant ownership to the cartoonists—the name, the characters, and the likenesses—we would be creating a revolution among cartoonists, and that is what happened. True to their word, Johnny Hart and Mell Lazarus moved their strips to Creators as soon as they could. The legendary editorial cartoonist Herblock (Herb Block) of *The Washington Post* joined us as well.

But those early days were anything but luxurious. I started with a desk and a phone, flying coach, eating at my desk, working 'round the clock. But gradually, with grit, we prevailed. In 1988, we started syndicating one of the funniest panel cartoonists of all time—Leigh Rubin—creator of *Rubes*® (and this book).

Creators Syndicate became a major success story and changed an entire industry—all because we connected the dots by listening to what was *really* bothering the cartoonists and giving them what they wanted.

Rick Newcombe is the founder and chairman of Creators Syndicate and has syndicated the *Rubes*® cartoon since 1989. Newcombe is also the cofounder, with his son Jack, of Creators Publishing, which has published numerous bestselling books. In addition to *Rubes*®, Creators has syndicated *Wizard of Id*, *B.C.*, *Archie*, *Mickey Mouse*, *Donald Duck*, *Batman*, *Zorro*, *Momma*, *Andy Capp*, *One Big Happy*, *The Other Coast*, *Agnes*, *Heathcliff*, *Herb and Jamaal*, and dozens of other comic strips. The company also syndicates and publishes many of the bestselling writers and political cartoonists in the country. And yes, Rick Newcombe also is proud to count Leigh Rubin as a friend.

High Rental and Getting Sentimental

Amisha Padnani

Sometimes, to solve a problem, we have to re-consider how we perceive a situation. Some years back, I was in a bind: I loved the apartment I was living in, but I could no longer afford the rent. I ultimately found a solution, but it required breaking out of my old way of thinking.

To give you some background, I was born and raised in Queens, New York. Manhattan was the place to be, and yet it always felt just out of reach, like I was the drooling donkey and Man-hattan was the carrot dangling just past my nose.

I decided that when I was older, I would live and work in Manhattan and have a sophisticated New Yorker lifestyle, dashing in a yellow taxi from my high-rise apartment building to the skyscraper where I worked.

Just a few years out of college, I had almost reached my goal. I was *living* in Manhattan, but I was *working* on Staten Island, where I was a re-porter at the *Staten Island Advance*. I loved my apartment. I was near Wall Street, and as soon as I walked out the door, I was swept into the energy of the city, nearly getting stampeded by people in business suits rushing to work amid a cacophony of honking horns. I would leave it all behind a few minutes later, boarding the Staten Island Ferry to get to the newsroom.

This was early in my career, in the perpetually on-the-verge-of-collapse journalism industry. To avoid layoffs, the company imposed a tempo-rary pay cut on employees.

At the same time, the lease on my apartment was almost up. The rent was being increased by $600 a month, and my roommate was leaving to go to grad school. I really, really didn't want to move. Maybe, I thought, I could find a new roommate who could afford the bulk of the in-crease and who could take the bigger bedroom. I posted an ad on Craigslist and exchanged a few emails with Cathy. Cathy worked as a corrections officer for the federal court system and carried a gun. She also had three large dogs. We met for pizza.

Cathy wasn't all that chatty, but she was friendly enough. Rather than keep either of our apartments, we decided we would look at some new places in the same neighborhood and get a fresh start together. The options in our price range were glum. The best one was a large studio that had been converted into two bedrooms. One bedroom was a palace; the other, a jail cell with no windows that very likely violated a fire code. With my salary, it was clear which room I would get. And even then, the rent was more than I could afford.

In the back of my mind, I knew I had one other option: I could move to Staten Island, where the rent was much lower, and I wouldn't need a roommate. I hesitated. Anyone in New York knows that Staten Island is the uncool borough—"the forgotten stepsister," my coworkers called it.

And, yet, time was running out.

I finally decided to take a peek at three one-bedroom apartments on Staten Island. If they were all terrible, I told myself, then I would go back to searching in Manhattan.

The first apartment was in a basement and had little natural light. It was pretty depressing. The second apartment had evidence of a bug problem. Gross. The third one was bright, big, and airy. It was on the second floor of a house, and the landlady, who lived below, was a sweet eighty-seven-year-old woman who loved to garden. From the kitchen window, I could see the fruits of her efforts—lush, bright green grass and glorious blooming purple flowers. The apartment was somewhat dated, but humble and cozy. It was perfect.

But…could I really leave the glitz of Manhattan? I couldn't make up my mind. I hemmed and I hawed and went over all the pros and cons. I talked to people I knew on Staten Island who had made the big move from Manhattan, but it didn't help.

Then one day I realized the solution to my problem. It was acceptance. I simply had to be willing to accept the change and whatever came with it. This would be a new adventure, I told myself.

So I took the leap. I enjoyed a ten-minute commute to work, and I joined a local running club, where I easily made friends. Sometimes I would see my wonderful landlady pulling out of the driveway in her twenty-year-old Toyota Tercel. She'd lower the window to say hello. "I'm going to visit my daughter!" she'd say, wearing her round, heavily tinted sunglasses. I'd imagine her turning up the volume to "Bad to the Bone" as she rounded the corner, even though she had told me the glasses were for her cataracts, not for looking cool.

I had found the one thing that I didn't have in Manhattan: a sense of community.

Six months later, I got a job offer in Manhattan as an editor at *The New York Times*, but I loved Staten Island so much that I stayed for another five years.

Manhattan wasn't going anywhere, I knew; I could move back, and, eventually, I did. But at times I yearn for the warmth of Staten Island. Sometimes I'll go back, and I'll run into a friend in the park or at a market. It's nice to know that Staten Island will always be there, too.

Amisha Padnani is an obituaries editor at *The New York Times*, where some people simply refer to her as "the Angel of Death." She counts as her successes starting the Overlooked column, about remarkable people in history who were not recognized; occasionally being an eight-ball pool shark; and completing marathons without tripping over her own feet. One day she hopes to learn how to properly pot a plant.

"What the...? Another rent increase?! How can they get away with charging us this much for a vermin-infested hole in the wall?!"

One Head and Many Hats

Robin Blakely

At a critical stage early in my career, I had an incredible sink-or-swim moment.

I was working hard to grow my own business and secure clients. But I was struggling and juggling to make ends meet. On one particularly difficult day, I found myself wondering how I could possibly keep it together. The way I saw it, I had two big problems.

The first problem was I wore way too many hats.

The second problem was I didn't know what to do about the first problem.

That's when something magical happened. Across the room, a little ray of sunshine caught my eye. On the kitchen windowsill was a vintage spice set that was comprised of six little glass bakers wearing tiny chef hats. About three inches tall, they were designed to hold spices, but I had always ignored that part about them. Instead, they served as cheery ornaments to brighten the space above the kitchen sink. They were a tiny chorus of supporters whenever I washed the dishes—a tedious chore I didn't like to do alone.

This time, when my gaze swept across the smiling glass figurines, I saw something different about them. I noticed their hats. Salt. Pepper. Paprika. I never before had paid attention to the names on their hats. Cinnamon. Cloves. Allspice.

My heart was pounding.

Six of them. Six Hats. Each hat had a name. Somehow, I had never thought of these hats separately. But now, their names made me view them as individuals.

Although they looked alike, each hat had a different name and a specific purpose. Plus, the set was restricted to a total of six. So, if you needed more than the six chosen spices, forget about it. These six were designed to get the main business of cooking done.

I thought to myself: The hats I have been wearing can have names, too.

I took a deep breath. If I define all the hats I have been wearing, I can tame them. I can limit them. I can prioritize them. I can understand them.

I got paper, scissors, and tape and made tiny labels. Cinnamon, Salt, Pepper, you have been renamed and promoted! Paprika, Allspice, Cloves, welcome to my business. The Six Hats moved from my kitchen windowsill to my desk that day. And I took command of my business and the businesses of my clients in a way that I had never felt empowered to do before.

My Six Hats were renamed Creative, PR, Marketing, Sales, Bookkeeping, and Traffic Management.

Eventually my Six Hats became the core of the coaching philosophy for my little company. They provided an infrastructure and method that I eventually trademarked and wrote a book about.

Today, those Six Hats live above my desk like a tiny chorus of encouraging supporters.

Whenever I look up, I smile at them—and they smile back at me.

Too many kooks spoiling the broth

Robin Blakely got her creative start as that funny little kid who believed that the thoughts zooming through her head deserved to come to life in words, drawings, and on gameboards so that others could play. She still believes that fun is powerful, and that talent means business. Now, a top brand-building coach and the founder of Creative Center of America, Robin helps people make professional dreams happen—faster.

An Eraser Is Your Best Friend

Leigh Rubin

My daily morning workout routine: Pencil. Erase. Pencil. Erase. Pencil. Erase. Pencil. Erase. Not exactly an aerobic or strength-building workout.

The truth is, I spend a lot more time erasing than I do drawing. My wrist is quite fit.

The eraser is my best and most frequently visited friend, but my second-best friend is my father's 1950s' Boston Champion hand-crank pencil sharpener. (Thanks, Dad!)

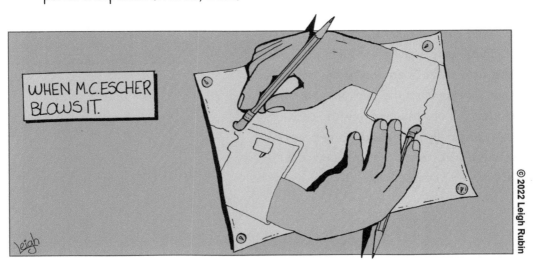

Sometimes I can mentally picture exactly what I want to put down on paper, but my pencil (always blame the pencil) refuses to cooperate. The perspective may be off, or the angle just isn't quite right. Whatever the reason, sometimes a drawing just "isn't meeting or exceeding expectations."

All these "false starts" are "rough drafts." If you never put pencil to paper, then you'll never have anything to erase. (Say, this could be a metaphor for life, couldn't it?)

Sometimes an idea sketched out on paper just isn't working. Big deal. There are lots more ideas. Sometimes an idea may be a great concept but there's something missing. In that case it goes into the very tall (and getting taller each year) "pending" pile. Occasionally I poke through that pile and spot the proverbial "diamond in the rough." Whatever was missing from the original sketch has suddenly made itself obvious, and now the cartoon works as it was originally conceived. Sometimes all that's needed is a visit from my best friend to help provide a little fresh perspective.

162

When Wood Meets Metal, and Stupidity

James Jepsen

Back in the early 1980s, we lived in a housing tract bordered by enormous old-growth eucalyptus trees. When I say old growth, I mean 75-feet-tall, creaking, dirty trees. Every winter storm season gave us more reasons to worry that one of them would wind up crashing through the living-room roof.

One behemoth of a tree struck fear into our very hearts. This 100-foot-plus-tall specimen of a tree arched over the house like a viper waiting to strike. Dad, an expert landscaper with many years of experience, decided it needed to go before the next storm took it down.

A long coil of heavy rope was heaved up into the tree with an air cannon, looped over some high branches. One end of the rope was tied off to a tree some eighty feet down the hill, and the other end of the loop was tied around the trailer hitch of our neighbor's 4-by-4 pickup truck; this formed a large "V" shape. Dad made some precision chainsaw cuts at the base of the trunk to ensure the soon-to-be ex-tree would fall in the direction he wanted. When he was satisfied it was ready to go, he gave our neighbor the signal to start his engine and start pulling.

Engine revved, wheels spun, chainsaw roared until finally...CRACK!—as the mighty eucalyptus began to sway.

"TIMBERRRRRRRRRRRRRRR!!!!!!"

The huge tree started to fall, away from the house. "Wonderful!" we collectively thought.

During the fall, one of the larger limbs caught an adjacent tree, spinning our victim around in a semicircle. This amazing, graceful pirouette was a sight to behold...until we realized it had been redirected to land....

Right. On. The. Truck.

Wood met metal with a resounding thud reminiscent of that incurred when stomping on an empty beer can. Thankfully, no neighbors were harmed in the writing of this story. You might be wondering where the stupidity comes in. Dad had mastered his craft; this was a simple mistake, not stupidity.

Our story has not yet ended.

The twisting dance the tree performed as it fell resulted in a rather awkward, five-foot tall stump remnant, three feet across. Dad decided that, as a strapping teenager, I should get my exercise and saw it down to ground level while he went to have a beer.

Now, being the responsible teen I was, I completely ignored his request and left the stump there for a while. By "a while" I mean eighteen months. Dad got impatient with my procrastination, so he did what all red-blooded American fathers do when faced with such a situation: He grounded me to home or school until the stump was down.

I certainly did not like this predicament. So I grabbed my Walkman, a two-man handsaw, and some gloves and headed out to the back yard.

I stared at the stump. The stump stared at me. I kicked the stump. The stump laughed at me. I grabbed the saw, incensed at this stump for just...being. This stump was three feet across, and I was using a two-person hand saw by myself. I was steaming. In my anger, I cranked up my loudest heavy-metal cassette to level eleven and went to town. I pushed and pulled that saw back and forth for the entire side of a cassette... nearly thirty minutes of sawing to a loud, angry, guitar-laden beat.

:: CLICK :: The cassette ended.

Breathing heavily, my anger now dissipated from the exertion, I stood back to see how much progress I'd made across the stump. *Six lousy inches!* I took a long, hard drink of water, caught my breath, and regrouped. I popped in my other cassette and pressed "play."

I started to work the saw with a renewed sense of purpose. The catchy, feel-good opening verse of Weird Al Yankovic's "Dare to Be Stupid" blared in my headphones:

Put down that chainsaw and listen to me
it's time for us to join in the fight
it's time to let your babies grow up to be cowboys
it's time to let the bedbugs bite!

I started to laugh out loud at the irony of the lyrics and continued sawing at a frenetic pace until the song ended. I looked down in disbelief and realized I'd just managed to saw through *twelve more inches* of the trunk during that *one* song! By the time side two of Weird Al's album ended, I had managed to cut completely through the remainder of the trunk.

With a grunt I shoved the trunk over the side of the stump and sat down to rest for a bit. I gazed at the tree stump, and then at the

meadow where the truck had become the first "heavy-metal" victim of this tree.

Then it hit me: All of the anger in the world is no match for a good dose of humor...or one ounce of stupidity. A very important life lesson learned, thanks to a tree stump, and one I carry with me to this day.

"Dare to be Stupid," indeed!

James Jepsen is a "jack of all trades, master of none." In an illustrious career spanning five decades, he has been a veterinary assistant, pizza maker, graphic designer, photographer, radio host, computer consultant, wedding officiant, disc jockey, and print-shop manager. Most rewarding of all is his full-time occupation as the daddy of an adorable seven-year-old girl who encourages him to find humor and joy in the everyday experience we call "life." As a fellow Weird Al superfan, she also continuously provides him with material for his lifelong career as an amateur humorist. James is on a never-ending quest to look at the bright side of life and make everyone's day just a little bit happier—or at least give their "eyeroll" muscles a workout.

Photos and Motos

Greg Kinder

A year out of high school, having worked as a wildfire crewman, I decided college might be a better course of action. I have the utmost respect for those individuals who consistently put their lives on the line fighting these monsters, and I was glad for the opportunity to work one fire season.

In high school, art made much more sense to me than math or history, thus my college direction was set! Through seven years at three different colleges, I received my master's degree in art and photography. Photography was my main field of interest. We were focused on black-and-white during college; it was the only medium considered serious at my school in the late '70s. The amber glow of the darkroom, the smell of chemicals, watching an image come up in the developer, and the lasting aroma of fixer on your hands was the best! My whole world was black and white, and I'd argue that until the black-and-white cows came home, and, to boot, I didn't have any Holsteins! For the next twenty years or so, I diligently worked and produced a large body of work that I was lucky enough to have been shown nationally in exhibits.

But eventually there came a time when I started to repeat my photos; I felt bored, like I was looking in the mirror hourly and seeing the same face. I needed to reinvent myself. It was time for a change. Color! My world needed to be in living color. Merely changing to color with the same images I'd done in black and white wasn't going to work; I needed a clean change of direction, but what? And to add to the formula, I'd been lucky to have an agent who facilitated my work and sales, which were doing fine. I didn't want to rock the boat too much. I tried a short experimental body of color work that was snapped up. But I'd mined that vein quickly and buyers were now wanting more color—yikes!

Around the same time, approximately about midlife, I decided to have a midlife crisis. Why not? It seemed to be the right thing to do and would send all my family and friends into a head-scratching fit. There was only one answer for me in my mid-forties, and that was a motorcycle. I'd owned a few bikes as a teenager, but now it was serious; I needed a big, loud beast of a bike! I took the plunge on Mother's Day, it seemed appropriate. I saddled up and rode away. I abandoned all reasonability and responsibility as daily I straddled The Beast and commuted or just rode on weekends. I was teaching part-time at a college about fifty miles away, so this became my primary transportation. Riding was pure pleasure—the air changes every few feet, the smells of the world were enhanced, I was in a 360-degree world of vision and experience, especially at night. *Wow-wee!* I had no radio, air conditioning, or heater—just my thoughts and the elements, stimulation beyond belief.

As I added miles on The Beast and became more comfortable riding, my thoughts and vision became more in tune with the world I drilled through, everything passing as a blur. At some point I realized I needed to get back to photography, but the wall I had built by changing to color was still there. I couldn't break through; lots of attempts, but no luck. After a year and a couple of months into this combination of midlife crisis and photographer's wall, I had a breakthrough. It was the Fourth of July, and I went out for an early-morning shoot at the river. As I walked and watched the river flow, I thought about riding and the motion of the world passing by, of the time between seconds, the time of stretched seconds, the in-between visions that you never really see. I started photographing and began slowing down my camera shutter to 16-second exposures to record that time. *Bam;* there it was—a new vision for me, and I found it on Independence Day. My independence day was a totally new direction that I felt deeply about, all from my midlife crisis and miles of motorcycling. And in color, too. Woo-hoo! It's been about twenty years since that revelation, a spiritual revival of vision and thought that has produced a large body of color photographs, which my agents have done really well, with plus a number of exhibits. Before buying the bike, I was not sure if I could break the barrier or change my medium to couch surfing. But The Beast delivered me to another world and, wow, the waters are fine!

Greg Kinder gave it up and retired at the ripe old age of sixty, since it seemed like a good idea! He studied art and photography in college, which developed into a creative life of careers and interests. Photography became his main passion, with a long list of national exhibits and collections to his credit, plus a twenty-year stint as an adjunct professor teaching photography. His day job for thirty-three years was working for the State of California designing, developing, and producing entertaining and educational exhibits, attractions, and programs. Currently, he is still photographing and also playing guitar, which seems to drive his cats into hiding!

"Wow, what a beaut! Do you realize what this means?!...The wind in our fur, our ears flapping in the breeze, our tongues hanging out and the freedom to drool all over the open road!"

Languages and Learning Lessons

Elaine Shein

When a coworker encouraged me to apply for a six-week Rotary Group Study Exchange to Chile in 1996, my first thought was, "I don't know any Spanish. None. Zip. Zero. Nada." I didn't even know how to say, "I speak no Spanish!"

No worries, I was assured. The first week would be spent at Berlitz's Language Center in Coral Gables, Florida, then, with a group of four other people, I would spend five busy weeks in Chile, often with translators.

I was cautioned, though, that at the different Chilean cities we visited along the way, the five of us would be split up to stay with host families for the night. Different families, every few days; some knew a little bit of English, but nothing guaranteed. I'd be on my own.

We also needed to do a few speeches each week—in Spanish—to Rotary Groups in the various communities. The speeches would introduce us, our homes, our jobs, our families, our seasonal weather, and even the natural resources of our home region.

I was relieved to hear that Berlitz instructors would help teach us how to write and speak properly for our entire speech, along with teaching us some basic conversational Spanish. Even though I'm a journalist, prior to the trip I had had a secret: I often became nervous doing public speaking. Like a lot of other humans, I sometimes felt butterflies in my stomach, trembled, maybe turned three shades green when having to do speeches. The thought of speaking in another language in front of a crowd of strangers reduced my backbone to the consistency of Jell-O.

And that's how I found myself, about halfway into our Chile trip, standing in front of a group of more than 400 Spanish-speaking strangers at a regional Rotary meeting. When another woman in my group showed her slideshow presentation ahead of me, some jokers in the audience said something in Spanish about certain photos she showed. The Rotarians roared with laughter at images that were not supposed to be funny. Those of us who didn't know Spanish didn't understand the jokes until later, when someone else explained, "Well, when she said she is a tour guide and showed herself standing inside a tour bus filled with old people, one guy said, 'I'll take the woman in the second row!' And when she showed how in winter it's so cold that you need to plug in your cars—and showed the extension cord leading to the car—that's when some guy yelled 'Is that so it doesn't run away?'"

The crowd was definitely in a good mood before I even stepped up on stage. I stood there, took a deep breath, looked out at the audience, glanced down near the side of the stage, and saw my small group—smiling with encouragement. Suddenly, I realized this wasn't a room of strangers. I knew at least a handful of people there. I also realized I had been practicing my speech for weeks now, and all I needed to do was read my speech carefully and calmly in Spanish, make eye contact with the audience, occasionally smile—and I could get through this.

My legs stopped trembling. My voice was clear and confident, and I delivered the speech better than I had expected. In fact, one of the people in the audience went back to his community—where we were supposed to go two weeks later—and told his Rotary group I was so fluent in Spanish that they could switch me from a family who knew some English to instead placing me with a young couple who only knew Spanish. (The couple tried to trade me back when my conversational Spanish ran out in the first five minutes with them).

I realized later that Rotary speech in Chile was a life-changing moment. I became no longer afraid of public speaking. If I can see even one familiar, or even encouraging, face in the audience, I'll be OK. If I can do my future speeches in English rather than a foreign language, I'll do great.

And, if I can make the audience laugh early, we'll all be more relaxed.

That speech was more than twenty-five years ago. I haven't been nervous doing speeches since.

Elaine Shein was so delighted when her first article was published, under a pen name at the age of twelve, for a kids' section of an agricultural paper in Western Canada that she returned to work as a journalist at the same paper for almost fifteen years—as an adult bravely using her real name. When she isn't traveling and struggling with foreign languages, she works for newspapers, magazines, and online/satellite media—mostly in ag journalism. She has done so for more than thirty-five years in Canada, the United States, and England, where she learned that the English language is *not* the same in those three countries. She still struggles with using both the metric and imperial measurement systems, and that weighs on her mind.

Norman never realized the unintended benefits of learning a foreign language.

Listen and Learn

Alan Ehrlich

We all know how important listening is, but, honestly, how much do we pay attention to *how* we listen?

I was always a good listener; at least I can assume I was. In my college days I had a radio show called *The Late Folk Spot*, and I always had a group of students who hung out in the studio when I was on the air. When the music was playing, they would talk about all of their problems—being homesick, difficult instructors, lack of a female student population (there were only two women in the entire freshman class—it was an engineering-focused school). They would stay for hours after I closed the station, just to talk because they needed someone to listen, and it seemed that I was their designated listener!

Many years later, my listening skills opened up an opportunity—facilitating focus groups for a local hospital. I was, in fact, hired to listen to the praises, complaints, and criticisms of the pa-

tients and staff and report back to upper management with a plan to enhance the praise and work around the complaints and criticisms. I soon realized that upper management wouldn't or couldn't listen to the complaints and issues being outlined without getting defensive.

So I developed a one-day training program that I felt could help them. The course was called Rational Listening—How to Listen to Complaints and Criticism and Extract the Golden Nuggets of Information. My classes included high-level executives, help-desk personnel, telephone-sales reps, and more. And I was off and running, teaching listening skills.

I thought of myself as an excellent instructor—dedicated to making sure that everyone understood what I was saying and attempting to answer every question raised. One of my signature moves in class was to walk right up to the desk of the student who had asked a question, have them repeat the question loud enough that everyone could hear them, and then provide my answer while I stood right there looking at them and making eye contact. A personal approach to classroom teaching!

Until a few of the students caught on…. "My listening Instructor can't hear!!! Can you imagine someone teaching listening skills who can't hear?" And the fact was that they were absolutely right!

Shocked! Embarrassed! I had no choice but to laugh along with the students at their startling discovery. The irony of the situation led to a few weeks of jokes and laughter. "My listening teacher is deaf!" Wow! But it also made me realize that I had to have my hearing tested and take whatever steps were necessary to both hear better and protect the hearing that I still had.

We always assume that when we listen to someone talk we understand what they are saying in both words and context. The same goes when we speak; we assume we are understood. Neither is true, especially when someone has an unidentified and untreated hearing loss.

In reality, my students' uncovering of my hearing loss changed the course of my career. I no longer taught traditional listening skills' programs. What I discovered was that you really can't teach listening skills without a full understanding of why some people cannot listen or cannot effectively hear. The concept of Listening Disorders took shape.

Since then I've authored a textbook chapter ("Why Some People ~~Won't~~ Can't Listen" in *Listening Across Lives* by Molly Stoltz, Karen Sodowsky, and Carl M. Cates) and lectured at a number of universities, law schools, and globally over the web. I've written a number of articles on various aspects of listening disorders, served as the president of the International Listening Association, and was named the director of the Global Listening Board and the Listening Disorders Division of the Global Listening Centre.

The joke, "My listening instructor is deaf!" changed everything for me and brought the concept of listening disorders across the globe.

From his earliest recollection, **Alan Ehrlich** wanted to be an engineer. He went to specialized engineering high school in NYC, but after a few years, his dreams were not being fulfilled; he was bored! So where do you go after working in microwave engineering? You become a magazine sports photographer—but not "ordinary sports"; rather, spelunking, glider flying, road rallies, kayaking, and more. This excitement was followed by various positions in marketing, computer programming, and even teaching. Now, at an advanced age, he has severe hearing loss and trouble listening, so that's what he currently writes and speaks about. On some good days, he even listens a little.

"Do you ever get the feeling that our god isn't even listening?"

Bossy Boy and Band-Aids

Frances Kolotyluk

It seemed like the perfect fit: We all had the same beliefs about children and classroom management, and the counselor was one of my instructors in the master's degree program I was taking part-time in university. As I left the interview for a teaching position there, I was sure I had the job. The classroom was in a beautiful old building with large rooms and wide hallways. As I was leaving the building, the janitor looked me up and down—all 5 feet 2 inches and 105 pounds of me—and asked if I was applying for the grade-three position for next term. I smiled and said, "Yes." His response, "You won't last until Christmas," would have deterred a rookie, but I had fifteen years of teaching under my belt, and they were third-graders, not hormone-fueled teens. How bad could it be?

My university course in classroom management showed research that birth order can not only influence a child's behavior, but also career choices. For instance, firstborn children, like me, are overrepresented in the teaching profession. My heart sank when I realized that of the twenty-three boys and six girls in my class, twenty-one of them were the youngest in birth order, who often want to be served, or only children, who are often not good at sharing.

Using a creative curriculum and applying the principles learned became my way of surviving what was to be my most challenging year of teaching. I ignored much of the attention-seeking behavior, the constant tattling from the girls, and bickering of the boys, focusing instead on the cooperative behavior I needed from my students. The atmosphere improved, and I made it to Christmas and year's end.

One day my most challenging student, Torrance, an only child, fought with a classmate over a pencil, leaving scratch marks on the other child. I could not let that go. In an effort to deny him an audience, I asked that he and I take it out into the hallway to talk about the incident. He said the words every teacher of young children dreads: "You're not the boss of me!" Clearly I had misread his goals; he was not seeking attention but had moved to power. He was right. I could not make him leave the room with me or by himself. This called for a creative solution. Instead, I sent the entire class out into the hallway with their work. They would not see a power struggle today!

Unfortunately, after I closed the door—with the two of us in an empty room to discuss what could be done—the assistant superintendent of schools, Dr. Al, who was just a shade under seven-feet tall, appeared in the hallway, to find my students working with heads down. My students explained the situation and went back to their work, and he headed back to the main office. They returned to their desks when I invited them back into the room. After telling me what happened, they were so angry with Torrance for "getting Mrs. K in trouble "with the "big boss of all the schools" that they refused to have anything to do with him for the rest of the day.

In addressing Torrance's need for power, his mother and I, with his agreement, settled on having him become the first-aid man for the class, dispensing Band-Aids when needed. Problem solved! Dr. Al and I used the incident to introduce my workshop on classroom management a few weeks later, and Torrance's mother and I still laugh about it forty years later.

Dick and Jane did not do much to motivate little **Frances Kolotyluk** to learn to read, but the laughter from her father as he read the weekly funnies did. Her love of the "funnies" continued and served her well in her thirty-three years as a grade-school teacher, counselor, and curriculum consultant and writer. Although Frances did not always ask the cartoonist for permission, as a Rotarian spotting just the right *Rubes*® cartoon for a Rotary fundraising event, she knew permission to use it was the right thing to do. Permission granted, and thus began an amazing adventure with Leigh Rubin.

Outside In and Inside Out

Steve Pastis

In looking back through the years, it seems that most of my self-proclaimed brilliant moves were later negated by innocent oversights or complete blunders. Whether it was a publishing venture or a career decision, when the chorus of initial accolades had subsided, I would usually be shown the door.

Although it was never important enough to be considered for inclusion on my resume, and it no doubt has long-since been forgotten by my fellow fourth-graders at McKinley Elementary School in San Gabriel, California, there is one decision I made that was never regretted and was never tarnished by time.

One day, Mrs. Gother, for reasons long-since forgotten, incorporated a coconut into her lesson plan. I remember that she somehow cut the coconut neatly in half and poured out the juice. She took out the edible part and showed us how the two halves of the coconut shell made a great percussive instrument.

Mrs. Gother made the shell halves go cloppity-clop, and then she gave some of my classmates the opportunity to do the same. I don't remember any of the nine- or ten-year-old aspiring percussionists displaying any musical talent, but occasionally the sound of a horse could be heard, or at least imagined, with a minimum of effort.

The class was completely engrossed in the current lesson, but their focus would soon shift. At some point in the proceedings, it became apparent to some of my classmates that Mrs. Gother would probably have no interest in taking the coconut shells home or even in keeping them somewhere in the classroom.

And so the frenzy began.

Fourth graders started shouting out how much they wanted the coconut shells. Hands were raised and waved frantically. Children leaned forward over their desks—as if being that much closer to Mrs. Gother would increase their chances of taking home the prized shells. All of the young students wanted the shells, except one: me.

"Steven, don't you want the coconut shells?" asked Mrs. Gother, perhaps concerned that one usually academically engaged student was bored by the day's lesson or perhaps trying to interrupt my classmates' shouting for at least a moment.

"No," I calmly responded.

Mrs. Gother seemed disappointed in my answer, at least until I continued.

"But I would like the white part inside," I said.

As luck would have it, I was the only fourth-grader in Mrs. Gother's 1963–64 fourth-grade class with any interest in what I've just learned (after looking it up to write this) is called the "copra," the edible part of the coconut. Mrs. Gother handed me the copra, then worked on the more challenging decision of giving away the shells.

I don't remember who received the shells, although I think she may have given each half to a different student. All I remember is how great the coconut tasted and how popular I was among the fourth-graders who followed me home for pieces of coconut.

My out-of-the-mainstream decision those many years ago remains unsullied.

Steve Pastis has written for a variety of publications, including *The Good Life, Greek Accent, Farm News, Custom Boat & Engine, Baseball Cards, Valley Voice, Circus, Rock Fever, Occidental Magazine, Cartoonist and Comic Artist, South Valley Networking, The Hellenic Calendar, Cool and Strange Music,* and *Gargoyle.* He has published three collections of his quirky short stories: *Fables for the Clarinet, Ten Good Reasons to Fix That Airplane,* and *Elk and Penguin Stories.* He doesn't get out much.

Cartoonists and Currency

Jerry Scott

One of the great things about being a syndicated cartoonist is that people want you to be weird. Expectations are very low when it comes to appearance, clothing choices, and general functionality. I call it Cartoonist Currency, and this is how I spent some of mine.

Jim Borgman and I were making our first European book tour, and we had somehow convinced King Features (the company that syndicates our comic strip, *Zits*, to newspapers around the world) to send us first-class. Don't ask me how.

Never having flown up at that end of the plane, we happily accepted every sumptuous thing the flight attendants offered us—champagne, gourmet entrees, French pastries, Swiss chocolates. And when dinner was over and the cabin lights dimmed, sleep masks, earplugs, slippers, and, unexpectedly, lightweight loose-fitting pajamas were distributed to all of us lucky folks. If somebody tells you that flying first-class is no big deal, they're lying. When dinner was over, the flight attendants made our seats into beds, complete with fresh linens and real pillows! This was a revelation for a couple of midwestern boys who were used to flying the middle seat in coach. But somebody else was paying for it, so we soaked up every delicious benefit we were offered, including one last nighty-night glass of champagne.

With our bellies full of French airplane food and bubbly libations, we slept until we were gently notified that breakfast was about to be served. Not ones to turn down French airplane food, we leisurely ate as the plane approached Charles de Gaulle International Airport.

As it turns out, it's common knowledge to everyone who flies internationally in first-class that, before final approach, you must change out of your pajamas and into your regular clothes to avoid looking like an idiot. Common knowledge to everyone but us, that is. As the cabin quickly emptied out, it became clear that we were stuck. Both restrooms were occupied, the jet-lagged flight attendants were giving us impatient glances, and our hosts were waiting inside the terminal to greet us. The only reasonable way forward was to spend some of our Cartoonist Currency and stride confidently down the jetway and into the terminal wearing airplane slippers and matching pajamas.

Cartoonist Currency: Don't leave home without it.

"I'm afraid there must be some mistake, sir. You're supposed to be seated in the *no class* section."

Jerry Scott is the cocreator of two syndicated newspaper comic strips, *Baby Blues* and *Zits*. In his non-cartooning hours he is a painter, exploring the landscapes, people, and animals he meets on the central coast of California. He maintains that living just up the road from Leigh Rubin isn't as bad as it sounds.

Glasgow Girls and the California Kid

Duane Degler

Years ago, in 1990, I found myself working in Scotland—a beautiful, generous, and spirited place. The work was in the whisky industry, so the many meanings of the word "spirited" apply!

I led a small team that wrote training materials and documented future work practices in order to implement what was then a novel and very complex computer system. We were one part in a long chain of computing being developed to produce, package, and distribute Scotch Whisky worldwide.

The project's complexity grew, as did the demands on my team, since we were tasked with creating everything related to documents and diagrams...of whatever type! Various small groups came under our umbrella, including the administrative team—three women charged with the logistics and communication for the total project group of about fifty people.

It was entertaining to the other team leaders that I had *all* five women on the project working for me—the three admins and two trainers. I think they believed that Yanks had different temperaments from the Scots' manufacturing engineers, who comprised most of the project staff.

Thankfully, the members of the admin team took it upon themselves to teach this young American basic Scots' culture, including many phrases and mannerisms.

It was soon a running joke when every day I walked in and was greeted with "Fit like?" (rough translation: "Are you well?"), and my response was, "Aye, fit b'daft!" ("I'm well, but crazy!"). It was the right attitude for that bright, spirited crew. Under their tutelage, I learned valuable insights, such as the range of interpretations of "Aye...," which were dependent on tone of voice; the cultural significance of old-school ties (my ties were abstract, colorful, "Continental"—receiving occasional raised eyebrows); and the underlying derivations of oddly named places nearby.

As the project progressed, the demands grew rapidly. We needed to publish hundreds of pages of documentation—with little additional budget for equipment or staff. This presented two challenges: How do I secure what, at that time, was rare computing equipment for producing in-house documentation? And how to coach administrators to become publishers.

The first challenge was to navigate the large corporate IT group. What could have been daunting was instead a delight. Not only did my counterpart in IT understand what I needed and why, she was married to a first-class chef who owned a beautiful waterfront restaurant, so our planning and negotiation sessions were relaxed and—for the food, drink, and camaraderie—memorable occasions. I would get my six computers (with—gasp—extra memory!), production software for graphics and print publishing (with the first generation of Windows 3.0!), and three top-line la-

ser printers (with—gasp again—extra memory!). In return, if anyone else in the corporation (not just the project, but *anyone*) wanted machines as fancy as my team's, then I was their help desk, so as not to burden the IT team. It was a bargain if not easily, at least pleasantly, struck.

But what of creating the publishing team? My three cultural interpreters came to the rescue, in grand form. One was very interested in art and graphic design, so leapt at the chance to "train up" in the then-just-emerging field of computer graphic design. Check! The second had a side business copy-typing books and academic documents and was eager to learn how to improve her products, making them easier to read. Check! The third, the head of the admin team, was our librarian. Super organized, she was most happy when cataloguing, proofreading, sorting, and shipping dozens of printed manuals to support all varieties of project needs. Check!

Sounds easy, right? Well, it didn't turn out to be easy when they sat down with their new computers. Everything they looked at, everything they wanted to do, seemed like navigating a strange, alien territory—because it was.

I struggled to answer their questions. How do we work with common styles, avoiding the natural desire to make odd things look OK on a page? Why do "windows" *hide* things and, for that matter, why do they sit on a "desk"? Can I swear at my computer because it expects me to know error code "MF3702b: unexpected boundary error" or "memory failure" (*Whose? What are you implying?!*), or at any of our myriad other glitches? And those cryptic icons...how do I pick the right one so I can put an image in that paragraph? Why is my carefully placed line no longer straight?

Then one day, as they say in Scotland, "The penny dropped." I realized I needed to interpret the culture of computer land for them, just as they had interpreted the culture of Scotland for me. I explained that everything they used was designed and developed by some young male on the west coast of the United States, nicknamed the California Kid. Together, we painted a shared mental picture of this quirky, twenty-something genius with a ponytail, in flip-flops and cutoffs, alternating between writing the code behind the computer's operations and playing ping-pong with his mates. The California Kid's worldview of office life (far from a Scottish factory), his ideas, his temperament, his values, and importantly, his *language,* was baked into the code. If *they*, the Glasgow Girls, had written a computer application and shared it, would *he* easily understand how to use it?

They laughed! They quickly realized that this quirky foreign thing was just another person's view of the world, and with this new power, they took ownership of it. It wasn't that they were stupid and those big beige boxes with the software were cleverer—they just had to learn a way of translating "young American" speech, perhaps into a new Scots' dialect.

They could do that! And they did. We all did. Our team successfully produced content and graphics and design to achieve whatever was asked of us.

That one idea, germinating from our early morning exchange of "Fit like?" "Aye, fit b'daft" not only changed our dynamic, it introduced many California Kid jokes in the office (the poor young guy was blamed for a lot).

Even more gratifying for me, as the project wound down a year later, the three women went on to successful and rewarding careers in graphic design, in medical documentation, and in administrative management. The best outcomes that they, and I, could hope for.

Duane Degler has a habit of encountering and embracing the unexpected. Opportunities arose that changed the trajectories of his personal and work lives, following curiosity and professional interests from various parts of the US to Europe and, a long time later, back again. Working in different cultures, practicing media, communications, training—and eventually merging all those things into the design of information and computer systems—feeds his creative impulses and the need to explore *Why?*

"Don't look so surprised, laddie. We can't all be Nessies. Some of us are Nestors."

Notes

The use of the nickname "California Kid" is a not-very-contextually-relevant reference to the 1974 film of this name, which is about hot rods and revenge. It has nothing to do with computers, but may evoke a sufficiently different cultural perspective. See https://en.wikipedia.org/wiki/The_California_Kid.

The use of the nickname "Glasgow Girls" is a reference to the boundary-breaking women artists of the Glasgow School, 1880–1920. It is not meant to refer to the human-rights activist group in Glasgow (2005), although that, too, is a positive reference. See https://www.oxforddnb.com/view/10.1093/ref:odnb/9780198614128.001.0001/odnb-9780198614128-e-73660 and https://www.nationalgalleries.org/art-and-artists/glossary-terms/glasgow-girls.

Crap and Creativity

Maggie and Dave Cox

For some reason, we thought it was a great idea to leave our well-paying jobs and start a small business. We're still not sure what possessed us, but we voluntarily jumped headfirst into a venture we believed would be good for our young family as well as professionally fulfilling. On Halloween, October 31, 1989, we opened a marketing, advertising, and public relations business. Our plan: build a company of creative people committed to quality work, with high energy and enthusiasm; financial and psychic success would follow.

We believed our business decisions should be made dispassionately, using well-reasoned data and a strong business plan that created a blueprint of our "big dream" for success. In our minds, business decisions were rational and emotions a distraction. And we mistakenly believed our past experience working in broadcasting made us ideally qualified to build a creative team.

We built a plan that was customer centric. We were all about delivering what clients told us they wanted. We didn't stop to think about developing original ideas that could challenge the status quo. Little time was spent getting to the heart of issues or brainstorming unique, imaginative ideas to achieve client goals. While there was no shortage of ideas, there was very little in the way of original thought. We were following, not leading.

It all came to a head one day when one of our designers appeared in the office doorway, totally frustrated and resistant to executing changes being requested because, as he blurted out, "I don't do crap" work. Space doesn't allow for a recap of the genesis of this statement, but regardless of the backstory, we were offended. Of course, we didn't "do crap." We were insulted and angered by the assertion that our work wasn't good. Once tempers cooled, we were tempted to dismiss the designer's tantrum as an overreaction and his comment as just voicing everyday work frustration.

Or was it?

What we realized, in our haste to satisfy the client's needs, was that we had overlooked the heart-and-soul attributes of creativity. We disregarded the hard work, the pressure, and the collaboration that generate great ideas and produce fantastic work. We were tone-deaf to the very personal vulnerability every creative person must risk in creating and sharing ideas.

Our eyes were opened. We learned that the best creatives are almost always independent, generous, hard workers who are willing to take risks. We also learned they can be thin-skinned, easily bored, rule-resistant, and mistake prone. Creatives are artists. They are sensitive thinkers who can rear up as bullies in defense of ideas. If you are going to create a great working environment that drives winning ideas, be prepared to take the good along with the bad.

At the heart of it all, creatives fear not being good enough. They fear talent gaps being dis-covered, looking foolish in front of their peers, being rejected. It's like that irrational recurring childhood dream of arriving at school in your pajamas and the panic that goes with the prospect of humiliation.

Oscar Wilde said, "A work of art is the unique result of a unique temperament." Every business owner wants to have a great working environment that promotes staff camaraderie and safety—and produces great results. That success begins with encouraging ideas and promoting the belief that every thought is worthy of consideration. Greatness is often rooted in a very simple starting point—one that must be voiced if it is to blossom.

We realized we needed to strongly embrace this value both intellectually and emotionally. Confidence to share ideas without judgment became our new reality.

We changed our thinking. We worked with our team to revise our mission and values statements. We wanted to make a statement that wasn't cliché, but which said it all. We wanted to reflect the beliefs, philosophies, and principles needed to push for high achievement, while, at the same time, maintain a healthy perspective in which all contributions were welcomed.

Mostly, we wanted our people to have fun.

In the end, we created a simple mission statement: Think. Create. Solve. Together.

Four words that don't say anything about writing good copy, outputting great design, providing outstanding photography. Nothing about increasing market share or building a new brand.

What they do say is that creative thinking is welcomed here. And nearly three decades and many lessons later, we are proud and gratified to have worked with some of the most talented writers, designers, and photographers in the business. We've created a long list of award-winning projects. We didn't do crap.

In retrospect, the irrational act of starting our own business was almost as fulfilling as having kids—and certainly called for many of the same skills.

Call it a shared love of black-and-white TV shows that brought **Dave** and **Maggie Cox** together. The facts in brief: a small-market California TV station: Dave, a management hotshot with a journalism background; Maggie, a marketer. Great success, great fun, and sparks eventually flew. A move, marriage, and kids followed, and then a "let's do our own thing" marketing and PR firm rooted in a second mortgage. All good decisions: forty years of marriage, thirty years of growing a company that was happily sold in 2018. Retirement!

Plan "Bee"

Leigh Rubin

There's nothing quite like the satisfaction of meeting a cartoon deadline.

There's nothing so frustrating as receiving a note back from your editor telling you that a cartoon might have to be replaced and/or a substitute offered, as it might offend readers or might be (mis)interpreted in such a way that could be seen as promoting an unhealthy behavior, like smoking.

At one time smoking, drinking, and guns were perfectly acceptable for newspaper funny pages. No more.

Newspaper readers, or at least a certain segment of newspaper readers, have become more sensitive and are bound to take offense at almost anything. Cartoonists are supposed to figure out *exactly* what subjects to avoid to prevent hateful emails or even worse, cancellation from any particular newspaper.

So, when my editor informed me, via email, that I should offer another cartoon because some readers might object to the cartoon because it could be viewed to promote smoking, my first reaction was, "That's bull****!" (In cartoon cursing, "&%$#!")

It's a fact. Smoking calms bees.

I put a lot of thought and effort into each cartoon, and the thought of having to pull it for an imagined transgression is majorly offensive.

Now, I like my editor, and I know he was only doing his job to protect me from the wrath of readers or from that of editors having to deal with upset readers, so I did my best to calm down (no, not with a cigarette) and see if maybe I could come up with a workaround to save the cartoon.

It was ridiculous. How could anyone even remotely think that the cartoon was promoting smoking?

While it's true that beekeepers use a device called a bee smoker to puff smoke into the beehives, this smoke does not harm the bees; it's only used to keep the bees calm by "masking" their sense of smell and prevents them from becoming agitated while the beekeeper inspects or performs tasks around the hive.

Bee smokers contain no tobacco. Different kind of smoke, same calming effect as tobacco has on humans.

Anyone with rudimentary knowledge of beekeeping would get the joke.

How could I work around the "no smoking" rule?

The answer was surprisingly simple. Why not place a "warning label" on the cartoon? This would satisfy the "easily offended" and, at the same time, playfully poke fun at them.

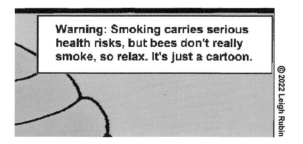

My editor loved the idea, and any potential blowback from readers instantly went up in smoke.

Girl Scouts and Goldfish

Kathy Medley

When I lived in Juneau, Alaska, I was finance chair for the board of directors of the Tongass Alaska Girl Scout Council. Raising money for a nonprofit is difficult no matter where or when, but in a small town that is landlocked, it is very hard. You simply cannot copy other fund raisers that are successful elsewhere, such as golf tournaments. So, you have to get creative.

The Territorial Sportsmen—a local philanthropic organization that supports recreational cabin construction, shooting sports, and more—also sponsors the Golden North Salmon Derby every year. In this derby, fisherman pay entry fees to fish for Coho and King salmon, hoping to catch the big one. On the day of the event, fishermen check in at a few "weigh stations" before going out to their favorite fishing spots. Previously tagged salmon, if caught, fetch big cash prizes. All salmon caught and weighed in become property of the TS and are later sold to cold storage for smoking or canning. It is a very big deal, and the event brings in a boatload of money for the TS to give away in scholarships. It occurred to me that I could copy that event to raise money for Girl Scouts! How? By having a Girl Scout "Gold" Fishing Derby. No, we were not fishing for goldfish; we were fishing for gold (aka money)!

The local hotel agreed to have us set up a booth in their lobby and provided us with a phone for our "weigh station." Press releases and invitations went out to previous donors, local businesses, and Girl Scout families. Fishers of gold could bring in pledges or checks to the hotel weigh station or simply call in their pledges. Of course, Girl Scout cookies were served to everyone who brought in some "gold" to the weigh station. The event was a big success and was repeated for the next three years. That was a creative way of copying another fundraiser and, yet, quite unique.

Kathy Medley, now enjoying retirement, has dealt with many difficult times—armed with her keen sense of humor and creative approach to problem-solving. She has a reputation for giving cartoons to doctors (about medical issues), to pastors (about heaven and hell), and to Girl Scouts (about cookies or s'mores). Many of those cartoons came from the pen of Leigh Rubin. Kathy's vast collection of cow cartoons inspired her password to be Bovine Beauty.

Circus and Science

Domenica Devine

"You were in the circus! Really? What did you do?"

I'm a scientist now, so if I want to continue to get invited to parties I'm going to have to lead with that.

As different as the two careers seem, it is startling how many parallels exist. My husband, Michael, jokes that the transition was "a natural progression." He laughs, but the truth is, they are remarkably similar.

Both—the circus ring and the experimental design—start with the seemingly blank canvas. In both cases, there are ideas, already half-formulated, half-dreamed, that are waiting to be revealed. The goal is to tell a unique story, one that allows the audience to imagine themselves in your lab coat or in your clown costume.

No, I was not the clown. Trapeze? Nope, not me. Rebecca had leotards covered in sequins, the adoration of the audience as she defied physics with her aerial acrobatics.

Both science and circus require extraordinary discipline. Performers must understand the history of what came before and improve or perfect those moves. Performers must practice the same actions over and over until it is revealed as elegant, effortless, and repeatable. It is a solitary effort, yet deeply dependent on teamwork. It is planned spontaneity.

When you work for a circus, that is pretty much the job. Of course, that's a contradiction. But it's also what brings a smile to your lips—sometimes with a gasp, as when Rebecca throws herself backward from her trapeze and catches herself by the ankles. Sometimes it is with a slow recognition of, "Oh, I see what you did there," as the clown trips over his own shoes to do a full forward flip to land on the balloon he had promised to a child at the edge of the ring.

But then there are the unplanned moments, when Jens sprains his ankle in the opening sequence, and his trampoline act must be scrapped. Everything must change, in real time, an ongoing creative improvisation.

We traveled from city to city, state to state, adapting our circus ring to each new site. Sometimes we were tucked under trees, alongside a river, or sometimes in a less hospitable sand lot. We would set up the primary-colored sidewalls early in the morning, arranging the bleachers to ensure that by the 3 p.m. show, the sun wouldn't blind the audience members.

We had so many moving parts, each dependent on the other. If one person was injured, others had to change their choreography to fill in the role. The adaptation had to take place while the band was playing, while the performers were performing. We were an extraordinary team, each able to imagine what could happen next, who could forego a costume change, who would hand the props to the jugglers, who could fill in the juggling act without the audience aware of the backstage improvisations.

Living that life of improvisation has informed my life as a scientist, and it did seem a natural progression. In my field of molecular genetics, there is an intense solitary practice. I have to know the history of prior experiments; I must examine the protocols and practices that will help me visualize the outcome of molecular interactions. I have to repeat experiments until they become elegant and effortless, and the data is replicable. Sometimes I recall these molecules as juggling clubs or as acrobats catching each other in mid-air. I have to be able to imagine their interactions, and, better yet, when new facts come to light, I have to adapt my thinking to accommodate the new reality.

While some of the hard work is solitary, it ultimately is dependent on teamwork. I am not the inventor of these ideas. Each lab has a dozen or so folks who are working on kindred experiments. These labs coordinate with dozens of other labs, exchanging ideas at conferences and through papers that have been reviewed by other scientists. We depend on each other to advance science as a whole.

While scientists don't often get the same applause as Rebecca, I do have some sequins on my lab coat. And on a good day, I am rewarded with the slow smile of recognition: "Oh, I see what you did there."

Domenica Devine has taken a crooked path through life. She has worked in the fashion industry, making everything from theatre costumes to haute couture. She turned left into stage management with the Pickle Family Circus. She used those collected skills while getting her degrees in molecular genetics and education. After working for years in biotechnology, she is currently applying both her circus and science skills to teaching biology at a local community college.

"Laughter Is the Best Medicine" study undergoing strict scientific peer review.

Crosswords and Last Suppers

Sean Sterling

In my late twenties, I became obsessed with crossword puzzles. I wasn't very good at them, but I felt it was a great way to regenerate some of the ol' brain muscles after years of resin build-up acquired during my six-and-a-half years at America's number-one party college. My Aunt Corky used to finish three different puzzles a day in ink. She was a law-school grad turned reporter turned politician, and I always held her as the pinnacle of a perfect person. Mimicking her daily habits seemed like a sure-fire way to get ahead in the world. After months of daily practice, I started to notice clue themes that absolutely stumped me.... In particular, anything remotely connected to the Bible. I'm not a religious man. I'm not anti-religion mind you...I mean, I grew up in America, for chrissake! My family did not attend any sort of religious services as I grew up, and, quite frankly, I've been blissfully unaware of its teachings, despite a handful of Judeo-Christian values picked up through sheer osmosis by living in the suburbs of Portland, Oregon. That said, this is a disadvantage when it comes to crossword puzzles. I could tell you the last name of the actress who played Joanie in *Happy Days*, but I didn't know my Hosea from my Haggai, and as far as I was concerned, Enos was a deputy of Hazard County. All of these words find themselves repeated over and over in crosswords throughout the universe, and for some reason I was unable to commit them to memory. I was determined to change all that. There were puzzles to be solved and, goddamnit, I was going be to my generation's Aunt Corky of the family. Rather than actually reading the Bible itself, which is a pretty thick book and has all kinds of esoteric vocabulary, I decided the best way to explore this new subject of curiosity (and keep it interesting) was to research artwork. I ran to the local library and devoured as many books as I could on the subject, eventually stumbling upon a video series by a Yoda-faced nun named Sister Wendy. She, in turn, turned me on to the "wowsville" of Leonardo Da Vinci. Yeah, I had a general knowledge of Leonardo. Artist, scientist, documentarian…. Nothing escaped his imagination, blah, blah, blah. But with focused study on his life as a whole, I discovered that he absolutely floated my boat. I had a new pinnacle of the perfect person. Aunt Corky was out. I was going to be my generation's Renaissance Man. I dropped the crossword puzzles out of my life and picked up the paint brush, hoping to ape my new hero's habit of staring into smoke and thinking wonderful thoughts. I spent a lot of time studying his *Last Supper* mural. Analyzing the hidden symbols, interpreting the colorful expressions, and dreaming up the conversations of the figures inside. Before I knew it, I had spent a good solid year of my free time recreating the masterpiece in a variety of mediums, with different pop-culture icons replacing the apostles, archaic superheroes from the 1940s in charcoal, breakfast-cereal mascots in acrylic, famous monsters of filmland in washed inks, P. T.

Barnum circus freaks in oil paints…. The ideas just kept coming on, and I was actually selling a few of my pieces to drunken customers at the neighborhood watering hole. "Woo-hoo," I thought, "This is my ticket out of the daily grind of schlepping ads to unhappy clients." This proved to be true. My last "Last Supper" project was the catalyst to my new career. It was a farewell present to a beloved coworker who was retiring. I had posed, individually, eleven of my co-workers at our work counter the week before, had my girlfriend at the time snap a pic of me in a "What happened?" pose, then Photoshopped us all together with Frank, the retiree, replacing Jesus. I framed the picture, wrapped it up with the Sunday funnies, and presented it to him in the break room over a coconut-flaked, grocery-store cake. Our VP of HR happened by for the celebration, spotted the picture, and flopped it over rather suddenly, fearing it would offend a particularly litigious holy roller who worked upstairs from us. He then grabbed me by the elbow, led me into my manager's office, and whispered in my ear, "Why are you driving a car for us?" Some phone calls were made, some resumes were floated, and with zero experience, I soon found myself in the marketing department of the eighteenth-largest newspaper in the United States. "Last Suppers" were out. My new walking orders were simple: "Get *The Oregonian*'s name out into the local community as frequently as possible. I had no one to impersonate on this one. I had to come up with ideas on my own. It's a decent gig. I've been at it for sixteen years now...and I have crossword puzzles, Biblical ignorance, and Leonardo to thank for it.

Sean Sterling is the community relations manager for The Oregonian Media Group, where he is responsible for securing and overseeing strategic partnerships with nonprofits and public events throughout the state of Oregon. Using a fake voice each time, he has emceed more than 300 rock concerts throughout the past decade. His underground lair is stuffed to the gills with comic books, empty coffee mugs, and vintage action figures. He insists he is not a hoarder, but his wife will tell you otherwise.

ASL and Appetite

Katiedid Langrock

In tenth grade, I opted out of taking a typical foreign language (if you consider nearly failing French for the third time "opting out") and took an introductory American Sign Language class. I'd been teaching myself ASL since I borrowed the book "The Joy of Signing" from the library at age eight. This would be an easy A. And it mostly was, with the exception of my midterm. Nearly all of our final grade was wrapped into the midterm presentation, for which we had to go in front of the class and sign a story based on whatever topic the teacher gave us that morning. I was assigned "favorite breakfast" as my topic. No sweat.

When it was my time to present before the class, our principal walked in to observe. The pressure was on, but I wasn't worried. I began signing about my favorite breakfast—French toast with melted cheese on top. In an effort to get the best grade possible, I decided to ham up the situation by not just talking about my favorite breakfast food but also telling a story about one time when I was absolutely starving and nothing would satiate my hunger.

In ASL, you repeat an action to show how immensely you feel it. So if you worked really hard, you perform the sign for "work" and then keep on signing it, over and over, using facial expressions and body language to get across just how hard you worked. Same applies if you were feeling not just hungry but really, *really* hungry— or so I thought. As I performed the sign for immense hunger, my teacher squeaked out a laugh. She immediately looked over to the principal, who stared on, bewildered. I assumed my teacher thought my favorite breakfast food of French toast with melted cheese was funny. Plenty of other folks had commented on its oddness in the past. So I kept going. Hamming up my intense and longing hunger, I repeated the sign again and again as my teacher, and eventually my classmates, cracked up laughing. When I was finished with my midterm exam presentation, I felt sure I had done well but also a little uneasy with the laughter. Was I really *that* funny? Turns out, yes, but not for the reason I thought. As my teacher explained, I was not signing that my favorite breakfast of cheesy French toast was the only thing that could satiate my deep hunger; I was signing that my favorite breakfast of cheesy French toast was the only thing that could satiate my deep horniness. Oh, yes; much to my fifteen-year-old mortification, it turns out that unlike the case with "work," when you sign the word "hunger" more than once, it means not that you hungered a lot but that your appetite was more carnal. I had signed the word "horny." My entire midterm presentation was basically me talking about how horny I was—horny for my breakfast. Luckily, the movie *American Pie* had not yet come out, or I cannot imagine the French toast jokes I would have received. My teacher laughed so hard she cried, but she decided to give me an A+ anyway, leaving me with this bit of wisdom: "Sometimes when we repeat

a word, it loses its meaning. It becomes an invitation for something else entirely."

Decades later, I was in charge of a television writers room for the first time. Once again, I found myself standing in front of a room, all eyes on me, with the producers—in place of my old teacher and principal—mentally grading my performance. And I was losing control of the room. Once again, everyone around me was laughing but I wasn't sure exactly at what. I kept repeating myself, asking the writers for "ideas, ideas, ideas," but what I was getting was unusable—hilarious but off-topic, none of it PG-rated or repeatable here.

I thought back to my ASL teacher. In repeating my word, I had invited in something I wasn't quite seeking. I didn't want ideas; I wanted *an* idea. I wanted their best idea. I wanted what they wished our show would be, so I changed my word to "wish"—a word that, coincidentally, when signed looks nearly identical to the word "hungry." Each person stopped giggling and thought. We went around the circle and expressed the top wish we each had for our show to focus on. When we got around to the producer, she said her wish was to break for food. After the writers cleared out, my producer said how impressed she was with how calmly and simply I had gotten the room back in order and made progress by clearly stating my needs. Just once. "C'mon," she said, "I'm starving." And she only said it once.

Katiedid Langrock is a seasoned television writer, story editor, humor columnist, and television executive. She got to attend the Daytime Emmy Awards when *Project Mc²* was nominated for best children's series. *Berry Bees*, which she developed for television, won the Diversity Media Award for best kids series in 2020. Her work can be seen on Disney, Netflix, Max, PBS, Amazon Prime Video, and more.

That day, Koko learned a new hand gesture not usually found in the standard curriculum.

Perfection

Leigh Rubin

My daily goal is to create a whimsical, visually interesting work of art, working within the 3-inch-by-4-inch boundaries of space and of deadlines imposed by time.

There are specific guidelines in order to meet that goal:

A perfect cartoon depends heavily on the reader's own experiences and familiarity with our shared collective culture and invites them to contribute to the experience.

A perfect cartoon should be "evergreen," that is to say it should be able to stand the test of time and maintain its relevancy years into the future.

A perfect cartoon should never underestimate the intelligence of the reader (because, as we all know, comics readers are the most intelligent people).

A perfect cartoon should never be overdrawn and under-funny.

A perfect cartoon communicates concisely, using both graphics and text so that the reader will be able to "connect all the visual and textual and contextual dots," which will allow them to experience a very gratifying "Aha!" moment.

And, of course, a perfect cartoon should cause the reader to spray coffee all over their morning paper, mobile phone, or tablet.

But how will I know that what I create will be "perfect"? It's one thing to have a set of arbitrary criteria and another to connect with a large, disconnected audience who have their own ideas of what they consider to be perfect.

The truth is—I don't.

That's why I like the idea of *acceptable perfection*.

The best I can do is to assume the reader's viewpoint. If the cartoon satisfies the criteria above (and it makes my wife laugh), then I can deem the cartoon "perfect enough," and it's perfectly acceptable.

Another match made in heaven courtesy of LoweredExpectations.com

Deadlines and Mistaken Identity

William P. Warford

When you write five newspaper columns a week, you develop a new mindset—if you want to keep your job.

By "developing a new mindset," I mean an ability to see something interesting in the mundane, to consciously or subconsciously be on the lookout every waking moment for something that you can write about in an informative and entertaining way for your readers.

Writing a daily column is like running in front of a thresher—you cannot slow down or stop. Many columns are easy to find: Spend a day in a courtroom, classroom, or a police car, and something will almost always happen. But not always.

Sometimes things fall through as deadline rushes toward you. Sometimes the best columns are discovered right before deadline, and the readers never realize how much you had to scramble to find them.

My column evolved from once a week to daily because I worked as an editor when I started it. The boss seemed to like it and asked if I could do two a week, then three, until, finally, I gave up the editor post and wrote five columns a week.

I soon noticed that things I would have paid little or no attention to in the past were things I could turn into columns. A news item about prisoners being included in the US Census? That turned into a satirical piece about an imaginary inmate from our nearby state prison filling out the long form:

Q. Is this a house, apartment, or mobile home?
A. Big House.
Q. How many people living in your household?
A. 4,212.
Q. How many toilets do you have?
A. 2,206.
Q. What is the annual cost of electricity?
A. $763,242 (We have an electrified fence.)

One day, the thresher was bearing down upon me, and I had a couple of things that didn't pan out. I went home for lunch at noon—four hours until deadline. I got my mail, and there was my column idea.

In the mail was an invitation to the Cubberley High School Class of 1965 Reunion. Now, there might be column material in my high-school reunion—but this was not my high school. This was a high school in San Jose, California; I went to high school in upstate New York.

All the better. Clearly, they had the wrong William Warford. This was 2000—before everything was done online and before everyone hired professionals to organize their reunions.

Before becoming a columnist, I might have tossed out the invitation or maybe called them just to let them know they had the wrong guy. Instead, I decided to find out about the other Bill Warford.

I called the number and talked to a delightful woman by the name of Joni, Class of '65, one of the reunion organizers. She told me all about their high school and what things were like in 1965: Cruising the main drag was the big thing; 1965 was just on the cusp of the drug era in America; the Beatles had just become huge; some of the boys went to Vietnam after high school, and some did not come home.

As we talked, I knew readers would relate because everyone's gone to high school, and most have gone to at least one reunion. Nostalgia.

I ended the interview, and the column, with my main question: What about the other Bill Warford?

"So, Joni," said I, "tell me about your Bill Warford. Star of the football team? First in his class? Lead role in the senior play?"

"To tell you the truth," Joni said. "I don't remember him."

She offered to call around to find someone who remembered their Bill Warford. But I told her no; she'd already given this Bill Warford his column, just in time for deadline.

Bill Warford grew up near Rochester, New York, and his Plan A was to play center field for the New York Yankees. But even at age eight, he was savvy enough to have a Plan B, so he decided, just in case the Yankee thing didn't work out, he would become a sports writer and write about the guy who played center field for the Yankees. He spent forty-two years in journalism, in California and New York, working as a sportswriter, news reporter, editor, and columnist. In 2012, he saw the writing on the newsroom wall and realized he should have a Plan C because newspaper staffs were shrinking. He went back to school and taught eleventh-grade English for nine years, then went to Plan D—retiring and returning to the shores of Lake Ontario.

Stars and Stripes

Leigh Rubin

My job is to give people a reason to smile or, even better, provide a laugh. I am serious about creating silliness.

But what happens if I am asked to come up with a cartoon that is not supposed to be funny or irreverent or goofy and, instead, is supposed to show respect and reverence? Something completely out of character from what readers have come to expect from my daily offering of silliness.

In late spring of 2011, along with many other syndicated cartoonists, I received an email asking for a cartoon to commemorate the tenth anniversary of September 11, 2001, marking the worst terrorist attacks in our nation's history.

September 11 fell on a Sunday in 2011. All the participating cartoonists would have an opportunity to create a special tribute in color.

I accepted the invitation without hesitation and with absolutely no idea what I would come up with to commemorate such a solemn, historic event.

The deadline was August 1.

For weeks I fretted as the deadline drew closer. I asked friends and family for ideas...but nothing.

I was stumped.

At last I reached out to my friend Claire, an associate editor at the *Advance*, the newspaper of record in Staten Island, New York, for her thoughts. She presented some of the grim 9-11 statistics, including how many first responders from Staten Island had sacrificed their lives.

That's when I decided that first responders would be the cartoon's theme. How would I pay tribute to these fallen heroes, these *stars*? I needed something strong and patriotic to honor them. Claire suggested an American flag.

The *flag*, *first responders*, *heroes*. It all came together in an instant.

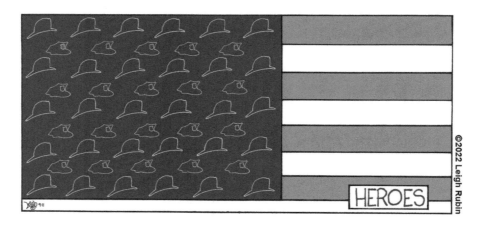

Colophon

Editor

Alexandra Hoff

Designer

Eric C. Wilder

Printer

Lulu.com